# OTHER BOOKS BY BRUCE E. DANA

MYSTERIES OF THE KINGDOM

MARY, MOTHER OF JESUS

SIMON PETER

THE THREE NEPHITES AND OTHER TRANSLATED BEINGS

GLAD TIDINGS NEAR CUMORAH

THE ETERNAL FATHER AND HIS SON

THE APOSTLESHIP

THE THREE MOST IMPORTANT EVENTS

STORIES & JOKES OF MORMON FOLKS

# PROPHETIC TEACHINGS

*on*

## DEATH, ANGELS, AND HEAVENLY MANIFESTATIONS

# PROPHETIC TEACHINGS

## *on*

## DEATH, ANGELS, AND HEAVENLY MANIFESTATIONS

### BRUCE E. DANA

CFI
SPRINGVILLE, UTAH

ISBN 13: 978-1-59955-491-4

Published by CFI, an imprint of Cedar Fort, Inc.
2373 W. 700 S., Springville, UT 84663
Distributed by Cedar Fort, Inc., www.cedarfort.com

LIBRARY OF CONGRESS CATALOGING-IN-PUBLICATION DATA

Dana, Bruce E.
  Prophetic teachings on death, angels, and heavenly manifestations / Bruce E. Dana.
    p. cm.
  Includes bibliographical references and index.
  ISBN 978-1-59955-491-4
  1. Church of Jesus Christ of Latter-day Saints--Doctrines. 2. Death--Religious aspects--Church of Jesus Christ of Latter-day Saints. 3. Angels--Church of Jesus Christ of Latter-day Saints. I. Title.

  BX8635.3.D36 2010
  230'.9332--dc22

                          2010040557

Cover design by Jen Boss
Cover design © 2011 by Lyle Mortimer
Edited and typeset by Heather Holm

Printed in the United States of America
10  9  8  7  6  5  4  3  2  1

Printed on acid-free paper

# DEDICATION

To my grandson Connor, who lived for a week and accomplished all he needed to do.

Likewise, for each of my dear family members who are in that special place called the world of spirits.

## A TRIBUTE TO A GRANDSON
### Connor Suel Dana
### June 3, 2009

Heavenly Father sent a celestial baby to this earth,
 The sweetest angel too,
And for such a tiny, little boy,
 We thought Connor had much to do.

However, Father knew he did not have
 Much time upon this earth to stay.
He allowed Connor a short time
 To feel love and hear his family pray.

Father sent Connor here to touch
 The hearts of those he could not reach.
He taught them courage, strength, and faith
 Because his life was so innocent and sweet.

Connor's tiny, little body
 Was so full of God above
You felt it when you saw him
 Because Connor came to love.

Connor had his daddy's big toes
    And his mother's cutest nose.
He had a perfect little body
    As everyone agreed, and told.

In seven short days,
    He managed what many never will.
When he went home to Father,
    Connor's purpose was fulfilled.

He gained an earthly body.
    He felt his family's love.
He returned to Heavenly Father
    In the celestial kingdom above.

When we miss him, oh so much,
I can almost hear Connor say,

    *My dear family,*
    *Though you wanted me to—*
    *I did not come to stay.*

    *Dear family,*
    *We are a forever family*
        *Because of the Atonement of Christ.*
    *We will all be together*
        *In a home that is filled with heavenly light.*

    *Thank each of you for your prayers*
        *And for your love.*
    *Know that I will be waiting to see you*
        *In Father's house above!*

—Bruce E. Dana

# PREFACE

Abraham, the faithful Old Testament prophet, speaks of our premortal life as our *first estate*. As intelligences, we lived as individual identities in this realm. Two thirds of the spirits who were faithful in this first estate earned the privilege to be born into this world and obtain a physical body. Therefore, life in mortality is called our *second estate*. Lucifer and a third of the host who followed him are "the angels which kept not their first estate" (Jude 1:6). They are forever denied a second estate of existence and will eternally stay as spirits. Those individuals who are born into mortality and by their righteousness "keep their second estate shall have glory added upon their heads for ever and ever" (Abraham 3:22–28).

From the scriptures and the Lord's chosen servants, God has revealed insightful and uplifting information about our second estate. The statements written in this work have been gathered from many years of research. Throughout this book, I have purposely limited my commentary, deferring to what the scriptures and General Authorities of The Church of Jesus Christ of Latter-day Saints have said on this important subject. It is my prayer that many people will find hope, peace, and understanding from the messages that are presented.

# ACKNOWLEDGMENTS

I am forever indebted to my wife, Brenda, for allowing me valuable time to research and write. I am most appreciative to my dear friend, Dennis "C" Davis, now deceased, who constantly shared his vast knowledge of the gospel with me. I am greatly appreciative to his son, Brian R. Davis, who is willing to share his father's research with me.

I am grateful for my scholarly friends—James Peterson, Meredith Bitter, Brett Butler, Matt Erickson, and Vaughn Cook—who have reviewed my writings and given valuable comments and recommendations.

# CONTENTS

CHAPTER 1

# OUR FIRST ESTATE

## "WHERE DID WE COME FROM?"

President Joseph F. Smith, then Second Counselor in the
First Presidency of The Church of Jesus Christ of Latter-day
Saints, asked and answered these searching questions:

> We want to know [on earth] where we came from, and
> where we are going. Where did we come from? From God [who
> is our Father in Heaven]. *Our spirits existed before they came to
> this world.* They were in the councils of the heavens before the
> foundations of the earth were laid. We were there.[1]

In total harmony with this statement, the Prophet Joseph
Smith said,

> God himself, finding he was in the midst of spirits and
> glory, because he was more intelligent, *saw proper to institute
> laws whereby the rest could have a privilege to advance like him-
> self.* The relationship we have with God places us in a situation
> to advance in knowledge. He has power to institute laws to
> instruct the weaker intelligences, *that they may be exalted with
> himself,* so that they might have one glory upon another, and all
> that knowledge, power, glory, and intelligence, which is requi-
> site in order to save them in the world of spirits.[2]

Therefore, all men and women who are born on this earth are the spirit children of our heavenly parents. This doctrine was affirmed by the First Presidency of The Church of Jesus Christ of Latter-day Saints (Joseph F. Smith, John R. Winder, and Anthon H. Lund) when they said "man, as a spirit, was begotten and born of *heavenly parents*, and reared to maturity in the eternal mansions of the Father" and "all men and women are in the similitude of the *universal Father and Mother, and are literally the sons and daughters of Deity*."[3]

## Defining Intelligence

With the limited knowledge that has been given by the Lord, we are informed that there are two stages of mankind's premortal existence.

*The first stage* involves a basic or primal element within men and women, which is called "intelligence" or "the light of truth" (D&C 93:29). Three scriptural references directly speak of this primal element within mankind. (1) "For man is spirit" (D&C 93:33); (2) "Ye were also in the beginning with the Father; that which is Spirit, even the Spirit of truth" (D&C 93:23); (3) "Man was also in the beginning with God. Intelligence, or the light of truth, was not created or made, neither indeed can be" (D&C 93:29).

Combining these scriptures, the Prophet Joseph Smith gives this explanation: "The spirit of man is not a created being; it existed from eternity, and will exist to eternity. Anything created cannot be eternal."[4]

In his memorable King Follett Discourse, Joseph Smith provides this teaching:

> The mind or the intelligence which man possesses is co-equal [meaning co-eternal] with God himself.
>
> I am dwelling on the immortality of the spirit of man. . . . The intelligence of spirits had no beginning, neither will it have an end.

> There never was a time when there were not spirits; for they
> are co-equal [co-eternal] with our Father in heaven.[5]

It is important to note that nowhere in scripture or any recorded discourse is this primal element of man designated as a living entity in the form and stature of a man or a woman. This primal element is simply designated as "intelligence, or the light of truth," and is directly associated with a substance called "spirit," which is eternal.

## Defining Intelligences

*The second stage* of mankind's premortal existence is affirmed in the writings of Abraham as recorded in the Pearl of Great Price. By means of the Urim and Thummin, this revered Old Testament prophet saw the great planetary system that exists under the government of Kolob. In addition to this revealed knowledge, Abraham was shown the organized intelligences in this spirit realm. In his writing, he declared,

> Now the Lord had shown unto me, Abraham, the intel-
> ligences that were organized before the world was; and among
> all these there were many of the noble and great ones; and God
> saw these souls that they were good, and he stood in the midst
> of them. (Abraham 3:22–23)

To differentiate between "intelligence, or the light of truth" (D&C 93:29) and the term "intelligences" used by Abraham as recorded in the Pearl of Great Price, we turn to Elder Bruce R. McConkie, then a member of the First Council of the Seventy, who wrote these clarifying words: "Abraham used the name *intelligences* to apply to the spirit children of the Eternal Father. The intelligence or spirit element became intelligences after the spirits were born as individual entities" (Abraham 3:22–24).[6]

Accordingly, all who have lived in the premortal existence are the spirit children of our heavenly parents. Though we do not know the laws involved, this primal element of intelligence was incorporated in the birth of male and female spirit children, wherein they became intelligences.

## Personages of Spirit

From what is written in the scriptures and the teachings of the Prophet Joseph Smith, we know that mankind existed as personages of spirit in our premortal existence. Eldred G. Smith, patriarch to The Church of Jesus Christ of Latter-day Saints, made this declarative statement:

> Each of us has a spirit body and a physical body. Before coming to this earth we were personages of spirit, *yet we were individuals. We could walk, run, speak, see, [and] think.* Our spirit body was made of elements not found in mortality. That spirit body, combined with our mortal body, makes a living soul.[7]

In another discourse, Brother Smith provided additional information about the ability and form of a spirit.

> Before we came on the earth, we were all spirits. What is a spirit? We use the word "spirit" to describe anything and everything, all elements that are not mortal—so we had a non-earthly body. *We were nevertheless individuals. We had the power and ability to see, think, act, make decisions.* We even took part in that great war in heaven, as a result of which Lucifer was cast out of heaven.
>
> *Our spirit body has the same shape and form as the physical body. The spirit body then has arms, legs, a head, and a mind.*[8]

## A Council Held by the Gods

Prior to the time the spirit children of our Heavenly Father were to receive mortal bodies on this earth, a council of the Gods was held. The Prophet Joseph Smith revealed the following knowledge in his King Follett sermon.

> "The head God called together the Gods and sat in grand council to bring forth the world. The grand councilors sat at

the head in yonder heavens *and contemplated the creation of the worlds* which were created at that time.

*"In the beginning, the head of the Gods called a council of the Gods; and they came together and concocted [prepared] a plan to create the world and people it."*[9]

The head God is our Heavenly Father. Again from the Prophet, we know that three separate, glorified personages comprise the Godhead, or supreme presidency of the universe: God the Father, God the Son, and God the Holy Ghost (first article of faith). We further learn that an "everlasting covenant was made between three personages before the organization of this earth, and relates to their dispensation of things to men on the earth; these personages, according to Abraham's record, are called God the first, the Creator; God the second, the Redeemer; and God the third, the witness or Testator."[10]

In this council, the Gods prepared a plan by which the earth was to be created, peopled by the spirit children of our Heavenly Father, and how each could be redeemed. The Gods first discussed this initial plan or blueprint of the creation (see Abraham 4–5).

## ANOTHER COUNCIL HELD

After this council was held, another council was held with the Father's spirit children to explain the items discussed in the council of the Gods. In this council, we were informed that an earth would be created where we would receive physical bodies of flesh and bones, and during our sojourn in mortality, "we would be tried" to see if we "would prepare ourselves for exaltation."[11]

## GRAND COUNCIL IN HEAVEN

After this earth was created, a Grand Council in Heaven was called. In this meeting it was announced that each spirit child would be given the opportunity to come to this earth and receive a physical body through the process of birth to mortal parents.

With a physical tabernacle, each would be tested to see if they would obey the commandments and teachings of God. By being true and faithful in this mortal state, each would have the privilege of coming back into the Father's presence with bodies of flesh and bones like His (D&C 130:22) and share in the fullness of His kingdom.[12] Says President Joseph Fielding Smith, then a member of the Quorum of the Twelve Apostles:

> We were duly informed that in this mortal life we would have to walk by faith. Previously we had walked by sight, but now was to come a period of trial to see if by faith we would be true to every covenant and commandment our Father required at our hands. We were informed that many would fail. Those who rebelled against the light which would be revealed to them should be deprived of exaltation. They could not come back to dwell in the presence of God, but would have to take a place in some other sphere where they would be blessed according to their works, and likewise restricted in their privileges.[13]

Agency is a glorious gift given of the Father to His spirit children. While in our premortal existence, we had our agency to keep the commandments and teachings of the Lord. In our mortal existence, this gift of agency to choose good over evil is essential in our progression toward perfection.

## PLAN OF SALVATION

From the time of our spirit birth in the premortal existence, we were instructed and schooled in the teachings of our Heavenly Father. We desired to become like Him. His plan of salvation—also called the plan of happiness, redemption, and exaltation—comprises all of the laws, ordinances, and doctrines of the gospel of Jesus Christ, and by conformity and righteousness, each spirit child could have the privilege to progress to the glorious state of exaltation enjoyed by our Father in Heaven.

God's great love for His children—both in our premortal and mortal existence—is eternal. As revealed in scripture, His work and His glory is "to bring to pass the immortality and eternal life of [His children]" (Moses 1:39). God's love for His children was to be accomplished in great measure by the atonement to be performed by our Redeemer in mortality on this earth. For as it is written in the New Testament:

> For God so loved the world, that he gave his only begotten
> Son, that whosover believeth in him should not perish, but have
> everlasting life. (John 3:16)

In order for the spirit children of our Heavenly Father to receive mortal bodies, they would be born of earthly parents. Thus, each child would become a member of a family in mortality. Therefore, it is evident from the scriptures, and the words of His prophets, that the family is central to the Father's plan of salvation for the eternal progression of His children.

Again, President Joseph Fielding Smith provides this knowledge about the Father's plan of salvation presented to His spirit children in the first estate:

> The thought of passing through mortality and partaking
> of all the vicissitudes [a difficulty or hardship[14]] of earth life
> in which they would gain experiences through suffering, pain,
> sorrow, temptation and affliction, as well as the pleasures of
> life in this mundane existence, and then, if faithful, passing on
> through the resurrection to eternal life in the kingdom of God,
> to be like him, filled them with the spirit of rejoicing, and they
> "shouted for joy." The experience and knowledge obtained in
> this mortal life they could not get in any other way, and the
> receiving of a physical body was essential to their exaltation.[15]

In this Grand Council in Heaven, it was announced that a Redeemer would be chosen from among the Father's spirit sons to perform an infinite atonement for all of the children of God. Accordingly, we could overcome physical and spiritual death and receive all of the promised blessings of the gospel. In this great family gathering, the Father asked, "Whom shall I send?"

(Abraham 3:27) From among all the spirit sons of God assembled, only two responded. Jehovah,[16] who would be known in mortality as Jesus Christ,[17] said, "Here am I, send me" (Abraham 3:27). He then made this humble but declarative statement concerning the Father's plan of salvation, "Father, thy will be done, and the glory be thine forever" (Moses 4:2).

Lucifer, also known as Perdition, the devil, or Satan,[18] responded as did Jehovah, "Here am I, send me" (Abraham 3:27). He then presented an altered version of the Father's plan. "I will be thy son," he said, "and I will redeem all mankind, that one soul shall not be lost, and surely I will do it; wherefore give me thine honor" (Moses 4:1). After the Father said, "I will send the first," it is written that "the second was angry, and kept not his first estate; and, at that day, many followed after him" (Abraham 3:27–28).

Due to the great gift of agency, the spirit children of God the Father were free to follow either Jehovah or Lucifer. Because of his rebellion, Lucifer persuaded "a third part of the hosts of heaven" to turn away from the Father's plan, and by so doing, they forfeited their eternal exaltation "because of their agency" (D&C 29:36).

After his altered plan had been rejected by the Father, Lucifer sought to obtain the power of God by rebellion. Accordingly, there was a war in heaven. John the Revelator described this event:

> And there was war in heaven; Michael and his angels fought against the dragon; and the dragon and his angels fought against Michael; and the dragon prevailed not against Michael, . . . Neither was there place found in heaven for the great dragon, who was cast out; that old serpent called the devil, and also called Satan, which deceiveth the whole world; he was cast out into the earth; and his angels were cast out with him. (Joseph Smith Translation, Revelation 12:6–8)

In a vision in this dispensation of time, the Prophet Joseph

Smith and Sidney Rigdon wrote:

> And this we saw also, and bear record, that an angel of God who was in authority in the presence of God, who rebelled against the Only Begotten Son whom the Father loved and who was in the bosom of the Father, was thrust down from the presence of God and the Son, and was called Perdition, for the heavens wept over him—he was Lucifer, a son of the morning. And we beheld, and lo, he is fallen! is fallen, even a son of the morning! (D&C 76:25–27)

From the writings of Moses, the Lord revealed the following:

> Wherefore, because that Satan rebelled against me, and sought to destroy the agency of man, which I, the Lord God, had given him, and also, that I should give unto him mine own power; by the power of mine Only Begotten, I caused that he should be cast down; and he became Satan, yea, even the devil, the father of all lies, to deceive and to blind men, and to lead them captive at his will, even as many as would not hearken unto my voice. (Moses 4:3–4)

Then, this informative statement about the war in heaven was revealed to the Prophet Joseph Smith:

> The contention in heaven was—Jesus said there would be certain souls that would not be saved; and the devil said he could save them all, and laid his plans before the grand council, who gave their vote in favor of Jesus Christ. So the devil rose up in rebellion against God, and was cast down, with all who put up their heads for him.[19]

There is only one plan of salvation. The Father ordained this plan. It is not the plan of any of the Father's spirit children. It is an eternal plan, and it was taught in the various councils held in our premortal existence. All were given agency to accept or reject the plan that called for a Redeemer. Those who accepted it were able to progress; those who did not, by their agency, were cast out with Lucifer. This glorious plan is called the gospel of

Jesus Christ. It is the only way that mankind can be saved and exalted. Without question there was a church organization in our premortal existence, even as it is found in the Lord's true church here in mortality. There in our premortal home, we were instructed and schooled in understanding and living the laws and commandments of God our Father. Evidently we lived for a very long time in our premortal existence. There, each of us developed specific gifts and talents. Individuals who are born in mortality as gifted artists, musicians, orators, and writers verify this, along with those gifted with a myriad of other talents. The greatest gift and talent was spirituality. Because of their spirituality, many were foreordained in their premortal existence to serve as leaders in the Lord's true church in their mortal existence (see Abraham 3:22–23).

## CONCLUSION

In 1884, President Joseph F. Smith, then Second Counselor in the First Presidency, gave this brief but excellent explanation about our first estate:

> We sang together with the heavenly hosts for joy when the foundations of the earth were laid, and when the plan of our existence upon this earth and redemption were mapped out. We were there; we were interested, and we took a part in this great preparation. We were unquestionably present in those councils when that wonderful circumstance occurred when Satan offered himself as a savior of the world if he could but receive the honor and glory of the Father for doing it. But Jesus said, "Father, thy will be done, and the glory be thine forever." Wherefore, because Satan rebelled against God, and sought to destroy the agency of man, the Father rejected him and he was cast out, but Jesus was accepted. We were, no doubt, there, and took part in all those scenes, we were vitally concerned in the carrying out of these great plans and purposes, we understood them, and it was for our sakes they were decreed, and are to be consummated. These spirits have been coming to this earth to take upon them

tabernacles, that they might become like unto Jesus Christ, being "formed in his likeness and image," from the morn of creation [on this earth] until now, and will continue until the winding up scene, until the spirits who were destined to come to this world shall have come and accomplished their mission in the flesh.[20]

---

## NOTES

1. Joseph F. Smith, *Gospel Doctrine: Selections from the Sermons and Writings of Joseph F. Smith* (Salt Lake City: Deseret Book, 1971), 93; emphasis added.
2. Joseph Smith, *Teachings of the Prophet Joseph Smith*, selected by Joseph Fielding Smith (Salt Lake City: Deseret Book, 1976), 354; emphasis added.
3. Joseph Fielding Smith, *Man: His Origin and Destiny* (Salt Lake City: Deseret Book, 1954), 351, 354; emphasis added. This inspired document appears on pages 348–55.
4. Smith, *Teachings,* 158.
5. Smith, *Teachings,* 353; the bracketed word co-eternal was in the quotation.
6. Bruce R. McConkie, *Mormon Doctrine*, 2nd ed. (Salt Lake City: Bookcraft, 1966), 387; the word intelligences was already emphasized in the quotation.
7. Eldred G. Smith, in Conference Report, April 5, 1963, 18; emphasis added.
8. Ibid., October 2, 1964, 10; emphasis added.
9. Smith, *Teachings*, 348–49; emphasis added.
10. Ibid., 190.
11. Joseph Fielding Smith, *Doctrines of Salvation*, compiled by Bruce R. McConkie, 3 vols. (Salt Lake City: Bookcraft, 1954–56), 1:57.
12. Ibid., 57.
13. Ibid., 57–58.

14. *Merriam-Webster's Collegiate Dictionary*, 10th ed. (Springfield, Massachusetts: Merriam-Webster, 2000), 1312.

15. Smith, *Doctrines of Salvation*, 1:58. The scriptural references used are as follows: "to be like him," from 1 John 3:1–3; "they 'shouted for joy,'" from Job 38:1–7; Isaiah 49:1–5.

16. Two of many scriptural references: D&C 109:68; D&C 110:1–3.

17. Two of many scriptural references: 3 Nephi 11; D&C 29:1.

18. One of many scriptural references for each name: D&C 76:26; D&C 10:12; D&C 10:5.

19. Smith, *Teachings of the Prophet Joseph Smith*, 357.

20. Smith, *Gospel Doctrine*, 93–94.

## CHAPTER 2

# OUR SECOND ESTATE

## THE LIGHT OF CHRIST

When we are born in mortality, we know nothing of the Creation, the Fall, and the Atonement. We do not remember our heavenly parents, the Godhead, the plan of salvation, our reason for coming to earth, or our desire to become like our Heavenly Father and His Son, Jesus Christ. A veil of forgetfulness is placed over our minds that conceals all that we previously knew or experienced.

Though we do not remember our prior life, we are not left without spiritual guidance on this earth during our probationary test of mortality. Every person is endowed with the talents he or she developed in the premortal existence. In addition, all mortals are endowed with a heavenly gift called the Light of Christ. At a certain age in life, every child knows right from wrong. In our language on earth, it is called a conscience. Through the Prophet Joseph Smith, the Lord says it is "the true light that lighteth every man that cometh into the world" (D&C 93:2). Moroni explains it this way: "For behold, the Spirit of Christ is given to every man, that he may know good from evil" (Moroni 7:16). It is called "the Spirit of Jesus Christ" and "the Spirit giveth light to every man that cometh into the world" (D&C 84:45–46).

It is also described as light, life, law, truth, and power. It is ever present everywhere. It is without shape, form, or personality. Yet it is the power of God, and it is the "light which is in all things, which giveth life to all things, which is the law by which all things are governed, even the power of God who sitteth upon his throne, who is in the bosom of eternity, who is in the midst of all things" (D&C 88:13).

There is a difference between the Light of Christ, the Holy Ghost, and the gift of the Holy Ghost. As has been explained, the Light of Christ is ever present and gives life to all things. The Holy Ghost is the third member of the Godhead, who "is a personage of Spirit" (D&C 130:22; see also first article of faith). The gift of the Holy Ghost is received after baptism and is given by the laying on of hands by one holding priesthood authority (see D&C 35:6; 55:1; Joseph Smith, *Teachings of the Prophet Joseph Smith*, 199).

Spiritual gifts come from God by the power of the Holy Ghost. Moroni gives this explanation: "And all these gifts come by the Spirit of Christ" (Moroni 10:17). This could mean that the Holy Ghost uses the Light of Christ to transmit spiritual gifts.

The Light of Christ enlightens every person who is born on this earth (see D&C 93:2; John 1:4, 7–9). The Light of Christ is also the light of truth. Accordingly, mankind is under the obligation to believe and seek spiritual truth. As revealed to the Prophet Joseph Smith, the Lord says,

> For the word of the Lord is truth, and whatsoever is truth is light, and whatsoever is light is Spirit, even the Spirit of Jesus Christ. And the Spirit giveth light to every man that cometh into the world; and the Spirit enlighteneth every man through the world, that hearkeneth to the voice of the Spirit. And every one that hearkenth to the voice of the Spirit cometh unto God, even the Father. (D&C 84:45–47)

Therefore, if mankind hearkens to the voice of the Spirit, they will be blessed and enlightened. Truly, the Light of Christ benefits all, but especially those who follow the promptings of the Holy Ghost. As such, those individuals in their probationary test of mortality will believe the gospel message and become members of "the only true and living church upon the face of the whole earth" (D&C 1:30). By study and by the Spirit, those members will come to know the true doctrine of the Creation, the Fall, and the Atonement.

## Natural Man Is an Enemy to God

In a sermon to the Nephite people, King Benjamin revealed this great truth:

> For the natural man is an enemy to God, and has been from the fall of Adam, and will be, forever and ever, unless he yields to the enticings of the Holy Spirit, and putteth off the natural man and becometh a saint through the atonement of Christ the Lord, and becometh as a child. (Mosiah 3:19)

Because Adam and Eve partook of the forbidden fruit, they experienced both a physical and a spiritual death. To experience a spiritual death is to be cast out from the presence of the Lord. All of mankind has experienced this death.

Though the Light of Christ is given to all—to know the difference between right and wrong, and good and evil—all do not hearken to the voice of the Spirit. Many choose to walk in carnal and evil paths; they go contrary to the enticing of the Spirit. Truly, the natural man is an enemy to God. However, by listening to the promptings of the Spirit, we can overcome our carnal, sensual, and devilish ways.

Though Adam and Eve experienced a spiritual death, whereas they were cast out from the presence of the Father, they were still given agency in mortality to choose good rather than evil, to follow Satan or not, to gain eternal life or eternal damnation. Thus, mortality with all of its trials and rewards was enacted by the Fall of our first parents.

But . . . I, the Lord God, gave unto Adam and unto his seed, that they should not die as to the temporal death, until I, the Lord God, should send forth angels to declare unto them repentance and redemption, through faith on the name of mine Only Begotten Son.

Then this important doctrine is revealed:

And thus did I, the Lord God, appoint unto man the days of his probation—that by his natural death he might be raised in immortality unto eternal life, even as many as would believe; and they that believe not unto eternal damnation; for they cannot be redeemed from their spiritual fall, because they repent not. (D&C 29:42–44)

## The Talent to Believe

From the days of Adam to our time, there have been a myriad of religious beliefs. In addition to millions of individuals who belong to various Christian denominations in this world, there are billions who believe in an assortment of other religions. Numberless people do not believe in organized religion or that there is a Supreme Being—even the Father and God of us all. In large measure, these various beliefs are influenced on earth by a common culture, tradition, or kinship. Because of the eternal principle of agency, each individual is free to believe as he or she will. Says Elder Bruce R. McConkie, a member of the Quorum of the Twelve Apostles:

Why is it easy for some people to believe in Christ, in his prophets, and in his gospel? Why do others reject the gospel, persecute the prophets, and even deny the divinity of Him whose gospel it is? Jesus said: "I am the good shepherd, and know my sheep, and am known of mine. . . . My sheep hear my voice, and I know them, and they follow me." (John 10:14, 27)

Continuing, he provides this explanation:

To this problem there is no easy answer. Every person

stands alone in choosing his beliefs and electing the course he will pursue. No two persons are born with the same talents and capacities; no two are rooted in the same soil of circumstances; each is unique.

He then concludes:

> Men are not born equal. They enter this life with the talents and capacities developed in preexistence.
>
> And as it is with the prophets, so is it with all the chosen seed. "God's elect," as Paul calls them (Romans 8:33), are especially endowed at birth with spiritual talents. It is easier for them to believe the gospel than it is for the generality of mankind. Every living soul comes into this world with sufficient talent to believe and be saved, but the Lord's sheep, as a reward for their devotion when they dwelt in his presence, enjoy greater spiritual endowments than their fellows.[1]

## THE STRAIGHT AND NARROW PATH

In the Book of Mormon, we are informed of a vision that Lehi and his son Nephi were privileged to see. Without relating the entire vision, a few items will be presented: Both of these righteous men noticed a rod of iron extending along the riverbank and leading to a tree where he stood. Beside the iron rod *was a strait and narrow path*, leading also to this tree. The tree, whose fruit was sweet and agreeable, represents the tree of life or the love of God. The rod of iron represents the word of God. The numberless concourses of people pressing forward toward *the strait and narrow path* leading to the tree seem to represent the people of the world whose intentions and desires are good (see 1 Nephi 8:19–23; 1 Nephi 11:8, 25; emphasis added).

Later in his record, Nephi revealed this doctrine:

> And now, my beloved brethren, I know by this that unless a man shall endure to the end, in following the example of the Son of the living God, he cannot be saved. Wherefore, do the things which I have told you I have seen that your Lord and

Redeemer should do . . . that ye might know the gate by which ye should enter. For the gate by which ye should enter is repentance and baptism by water; and then cometh a remission of your sins by fire and by the Holy Ghost. *And then are ye in this strait and narrow path which leads to eternal life.* (2 Nephi 31:16–18; emphasis added)

In the Book of Mormon both the words *strait* and *straight* are used. In the vision that Lehi and Nephi saw, they saw this "*strait* and narrow path which leads to eternal life" (2 Nephi 31:18; see also 1 Nephi 8:20; emphasis added). However, this same Nephi writes: "O then, my beloved brethren, come unto the Lord, the Holy One. Remember that his paths are righteous. Behold, the way for man is narrow, but it lieth in a *straight* course before him . . ." (2 Nephi 9:41; emphasis added). Thus, both the words *strait* and *straight* are written.

Three years before his death, Elder Bruce R. McConkie gave one of the most comforting and faith-promoting speeches of his life. In his talk, he uses the word *straight* to speak of the path leading to eternal life. Said he:

This is a true gospel verity—that everyone in the Church who is on the straight and narrow path, who is striving and struggling and desiring to do what is right, though is far from perfect in this life; if he passes out of this life while he's on the straight and narrow, he's going to go on to eternal reward in his Father's kingdom.[2]

Because of the eternal plan of salvation, God the Father and His Beloved Son, Jesus Christ, have restored the gospel in our dispensation through the Prophet Joseph Smith, which provides the only way that mankind can come back into their presence and become like them (see D&C 1:17–30; Joseph Smith—History 1:17–20; D&C 76).

With the talent to believe the truth, using agency to act for ourselves, by becoming converted to The Church of Jesus Christ of Latter-day Saints, and working by faith and works, we are on the "straight and narrow path" that leads to eternal life.

As has been explained, all who kept their first estate in the premortal existence would be allowed to come to this mortal existence, in order to obtain a physical body that each might become like our Creator, who is our Heavenly Father. Our mortal life is a test, to see if we will do all things that the Lord requires of us. For as it is written in the book of Abraham: "And we will prove them herewith, to see if they will do all things whatsoever the Lord their God shall command them;" if so, this great promise is given, "and they who keep their second estate shall have glory added upon their heads for ever and ever" (Abraham 3:25–26).

As recorded in the Book of Mormon, Alma made this important statement: "This life is the time for men [mankind] to prepare to meet God; yea, behold the day of this life is the day for men to perform their labors." Then, he cautions against procrastinating the day of our repentance and our faithfulness in this life. "Behold, if we do not improve our time while in this life, then cometh the night of darkness wherein there can be no labor performed" (see Alma 34:32–33).

## CONCLUSION

This is how mankind can prepare to meet God in this life: The Father of us all ordained and established a plan of salvation whereby His spirit children might advance and become like Him. It is the gospel of Jesus Christ, the plan of the Eternal Father, the only way that mankind can be saved and exalted. Our Father loves each of His children more than we can fully know in mortality. He wants us to succeed. Therefore, our great desire and hope is to find and then stay on the straight and narrow path that leads to eternal life (see 1 Nephi 8:20; 2 Nephi 31:18).

## NOTES

1. Bruce R. McConkie, *A New Witness for the Articles of Faith* (Salt Lake City: Deseret Book, 1985), 33–34.
2. Bruce R. McConkie, "The Probationary Test of Mortality," Salt Lake Institute of Religion address, 10 January 1982, 12.

CHAPTER 3

# SPIRITS LOOK
# LIKE MORTALS

## IMAGE AND LIKENESS THE SAME

Many members of The Church of Jesus Christ of Latter-day Saints have wondered if their premortal spirit resembles their mortal body in appearance. In a revelation given to the Prophet Joseph Smith in 1832, the Lord declared,

> *That which is spiritual being in the likeness of that which is temporal*; and that which is temporal in the likeness of that which is spiritual; *the spirit of man in the likeness of his person*, as also the spirit of the beast, and every other creature which God has created. (D&C 77:2; emphasis added)

Concerning this informative revelation, President Harold B. Lee, then a member of the Quorum of the Twelve Apostles, made this declaration:

> Now if you will turn to the 77th section of the Doctrine and Covenants . . . you will find in the second verse it suggests what a spirit looks like . . .
>
> *Now, think what those words mean.* Every full-grown person who lives upon the earth has a physical body which is the *counterpart* of the spirit which tabernacles that body. In fact, here the truth is given that all living things have their spiritual entities and that the full-grown or full-sized material creations are

the *exact counterpart* of the spiritual, the spiritual being in the likeness of that which is temporal. *In other words if we could see our spirit bodies standing by our sides, we would see that they have the same look, are the same size, have the same shape, and have the same identities.*[1]

An individual begins life as a small baby and over the course of several years eventually reaches the stature of an adult. For a variety of reasons, individuals on earth either gain or lose weight throughout their mortal life. Because a spirit is highly elastic in its nature, it has the ability to conform to the size of the physical body it is housed in.[2] Therefore, as President Lee has adequately explained, if we could see our spirit bodies standing by our physical bodies—at any given time in our life—it would have the same look, size, shape, and identity.

## Ability and Form of a Spirit

In another discourse, President Lee quoted the same revelation and spoke about the ability and form of a spirit:

> In other words, we have a spirit which our temporal body is shaping itself to. *Or, shall I say the body is being shaped to the full-grown spirit that tabernacles therein.* Our spirits have *eyes to see and ears to hear, mouths with which to speak.* We must train our spiritual selves with the same care, if we are to be fully developed, as we train our physical bodies.[3]

In harmony with this teaching, Eldred G. Smith made this declarative statement:

> Each of us has a spirit body and a physical body. Before coming to this earth we were personages of spirit, *yet we were individuals. We could walk, run, speak, see, [and] think.* Our spirit body was made of elements not found in mortality. That spirit body, combined with our mortal body, makes a living soul.[4]

In another general conference, Brother Smith provided additional information about the ability and form of a spirit:

Before we came on the earth, we were all spirits. What is a spirit? We use the word "spirit" to describe anything and everything, all elements that are not mortal—so we had a non-earthly body. *We were nevertheless individuals. We had the power and ability to see, think, act, make decisions.* We even took part in that great war in heaven, as a result of which Lucifer was cast out of heaven.

*Our spirit body has the same shape and form as the physical body. The spirit body then has arms, legs, a head, and a mind.*[5]

In agreement with this teaching, Elder Orson Pratt, a member of the Quorum of the Twelve Apostles, expressed this teaching:

I believe that if our spirits could be taken from our bodies and stand before us, so that we could gaze upon them with our natural eyes, we would see *the likeness and image of each* of the tabernacles out of which they were taken.[6]

Therefore, these statements adequately explain that spirits see and act and think. They have great ability to do things. Thus, a spirit has all of the parts of a mortal body.

In another address, Elder Pratt provided additional information concerning the identity of spirits:

When we occupied our first estate[7] [commonly called the premortal existence], dwelling in the presence of the Father . . . we were there as intelligent spirits, *in our present form and shape.*[8]

Speaking of the Resurrection, Alma explained that "all things shall be restored to their proper and perfect frame" (Alma 40:23). Because of this great knowledge, it is reasonable to believe that in the premortal existence, every spirit was also in its proper and perfect frame. In support of this belief, Elder Orson Pratt asked and answered his own question:

For do you suppose that God [the Father] in begetting spirits in the eternal world would beget an imperfect [being] that had no capacities? No . . . but it is because of the imperfection of the tabernacle in which the spirit dwells.[9]

In harmony with this statement, Elder James E. Talmage, a member of the Quorum of the Twelve Apostles, declared: "The perfect [mortal] body is the counterpart of the *perfect spirit.*"[10]

Paraphrasing what Elder Pratt said on another occasion, in our first estate, the spirit body was the same shape and form as the physical body.[11] This statement is in harmony with the revelation given to the Prophet Joseph Smith, "*the spirit of man in the likeness of his person*" (D&C 77:2; emphasis added).

President Joseph F. Smith explained that a son of Bishop Edward Hunter, who died when a little child, "came to him, *in the stature of full-grown manhood,* and revealed himself to his father, and said: 'I am your son.'"

Not understanding, Bishop Hunter spoke with Hyrum Smith, father of President Joseph F. Smith and brother of the Prophet Joseph Smith, and said: " 'Hyrum, what does that mean? I buried my son when he was only a little boy, but he has come to me as a full-grown man . . . What does it mean?'"

President Joseph F. Smith said, "Father . . . told him that the Spirit of Jesus Christ was full-grown before he was born into the world; and so *our children were full-grown and possessed their full stature in the spirit, before they entered mortality.*"[12]

From these statements, it is plainly taught that premortal spirits are full-grown before they enter a mortal tabernacle. And, if we were allowed to see our spirit bodies standing by our sides, at any stage of development in our mortal life, we would see that "they have the same look, are the same size, have the same shape, and have the same identities."

## Brother of Jared's Experience

Regarding Hyrum Smith, the patriarch, telling Bishop Hunter that the Spirit of Jesus Christ was full-grown before he was born into the world, we turn to an account recorded in the book of Ether. The brother of Jared went upon mount Shelem and melted out of rock sixteen clear stones, two for each of the eight vessels that had been built to cross the great sea. With this accomplished, he carried these small stones in his hands to the top of the mount and there offered a powerful but humble prayer (see Ether 2:6–17; 3:1–4). We begin by reading a portion of his mighty prayer:

> And I know, O Lord, that thou hast all power, and can do whatsoever thou wilt for the benefit of man; *therefore touch these stones, O Lord, with thy finger*, and prepare them that they may shine forth in darkness; and they shall shine forth unto us in the vessels which we have prepared, that we may have light while we shall cross the sea . . .
>
> And it came to pass that when the brother of Jared had said these words, behold, the *Lord stretched forth his hand and touched the stones one by one with his finger*. And the veil was taken from off the eyes of the brother of Jared, and *he saw the finger of the Lord*. (Ether 3:4, 6; emphasis added)

Then, these significant words are written:

> And it was as the finger of a man, *like unto flesh and blood*; and the brother of Jared fell down before the Lord, for he was struck with fear. (Ether 3:6; emphasis added)

Next, these marvelous conversations are recorded:

> And the Lord saw that the brother of Jared had fallen to the earth; and the Lord said unto him: Arise, why hast thou fallen?
>
> And he saith unto the Lord: *I saw the finger of the Lord*, and I feared lest he should smite me; *for I knew not the Lord had flesh and blood*.
>
> And the Lord said unto him: Because of thy faith thou hast seen that *I shall take upon me flesh and blood*; and never has man come before me with such *exceeding faith* as thou hast; for were it not so ye could not have seen my finger. (Ether 3:7–9)

## FLESH AND BLOOD

What does the expression *flesh and blood* mean? In the Old Testament it is written, *"For the life of the flesh is in the blood"* (Leviticus 17:11; emphasis added). In the New Testament the following is written:

> When Jesus came into the coasts of Caesarea Philippi, he asked his disciples, saying, Whom do men say that I the Son of man am?
>
> And Simon Peter answered and said, Thou art the Christ, the Son of the living God.
>
> And Jesus answered and said unto him, Blessed art thou, Simon Bar-jona: *for flesh and blood hath not revealed it unto thee*, but my Father which is in heaven. (Matthew 16:13, 16–17; emphasis added)

Therefore, *flesh and blood* refers to or means mortality. With this knowledge, we return again to the account of the brother of Jared. It is reasonable to believe that before this righteous man "saw the finger of the Lord," he knew the doctrine that "God created man in his own image, in the image of God created he him; male and female created he them" (Genesis 1:27). Previously, the Spirit Lord had spoken to the brother of Jared three times (see Ether 1:40–43; 2:4–5, 14–16, 23–25). Thus, this faithful man knew that the Lord was able to speak and communicate as a man. Therefore, when the brother of Jared exclaimed, "for I knew not that *the Lord had flesh and blood*" (Ether 3:8), it is reasonable to believe that it had nothing to do with the form of our Savior, *but that he was surprised that our Lord's spirit finger had color or pigmentation the same as mortals.*

## SPIRIT LORD SEEN BY MORIANCUMER

Regarding the unique experience of the brother of Jared, Elder B. H. Roberts, one of the first seven Presidents of the Seventy, stated:

We read of Jesus, the Christ, appearing unto Moriancumer[13] [the brother of Jared] upon the mount; and when by faith Moriancumer saw the finger of that spirit he pleaded that he might have a full vision of the divine personage of the Christ. The veil parted and the Christ, his pre-existent spirit, stood before the prophet, and said to him: "Behold, this body, which ye now behold, is the body of my spirit; . . . and even as I appear unto thee to be in the spirit will I appear unto my people in the flesh." From this we gather the fact that it is *the expression of the spirit that shines through the tabernacle; that if spirit and body could be separated and placed side by side, we would see then that the inner man had fashioned after his own likeness the outward man* . . . So that character, the nobility of it, the greatness and goodness of it in any individual case *depends upon what the pre-existent spirit was*—that is, what *the spirit was before it tabernacled in the flesh*.[14]

## Heredity

Though science teaches that people inherit their appearances and character traits from parents and grandparents, Elder Roberts expressed this view:

It is to the spirits of men, then, that you want to look for the determining factor of character rather than to earthly parentage—rather than to heredity.[15]

To support his belief, he gave the following example:

Excellent for purity, and standing in my admiration above all earthly women, is the mother of the Christ; yet pure and beautiful as I think her to have been she did not make the Christ. *She did not communicate to him the attributes of his spirit.* He was already the Son of God in the spirit world. He was, under the direction of the Father, the creator of this world, and doubtless of many world systems . . . As the character of the Christ was *primarily fixed* by what His spirit was before His earth life began, *so, too, the character of other men depends primarily upon the nature of their spirits in that pre-earth life where they lived in spirit existence.* So, I repeat, it is *with the spirits of men* that we have to deal *rather than with heredity.*[16]

Concerning the "spirits of men . . . rather than with heredity," Elder James E. Talmage spoke these meaningful words in a general conference:

> We had an existence before we were born. *In that existence you were you and I was I before our spirits entered into these bodies.* You will be you and I shall be I *after* the change called death befalls us. *We shall maintain our identity, or it shall be preserved unto us, through and beyond the resurrection, for we are eternal!*[17]

In total harmony with the statement made by Elder Talmage, Elder Hartman Rector Jr., a member of the First Quorum of the Seventy, said,

> Man is a spirit living in a house of clay called a physical body. This combination of spirit and body is called a living soul.
>
> Physical bodies are made of flesh and bone and, therefore, have tangible form and shape and are easy to see and feel and recognize. *The spirit also has a definite form and shape* but does not have flesh and bone and, therefore, is not easy for mortals to see, feel, and recognize.
>
> The scriptures tell us that the spirit and the body in which it lives *look very, very much alike*—and are, in fact, made in the image and likeness of God.
>
> The word *life* means that the spirit is at home in the physical body. Death, on the other hand, means that the spirit has departed the physical body. When death occurs or when the spirit leaves the physical body, the physical body decays and returns to the dust whence it came. *However, the spirit continues to exist in another realm called "the spirit world" and still maintains its form and shape and identity.*[18]

## SPIRIT IDENTITY

President Wilford Woodruff, the fourth President of The Church of Jesus Christ of Latter-day Saints, was personally acquainted with the Prophet Joseph Smith. Concerning his call to the Twelve, the following is written:

> While holding meeting with the Saints at North Vinal Haven, on the 9th of August [1838], I received a letter from Elder Thomas B. Marsh, who was then President of the Twelve Apostles, informing me that *the Prophet Joseph Smith had received a revelation from the Lord* [D&C 118:6], *naming as persons to be chosen to fill the places of those of the Twelve who had fallen.* Those named were John E. Page, John Taylor, *Wilford Woodruff* and Willard Richards . . . The substance of this letter had been revealed to me several weeks before, but I had not named it to any person.[19]

Concerning some of his unique experiences, President Woodruff declared,

> *Joseph Smith visited me a great deal after his death*, and taught me many important principles. On one occasion *he and his brother Hyrum visited me* while I was in a storm at sea . . .
>
> Joseph Smith continued visiting myself and others up to a certain time, and then it stopped. *The last time I saw him was in heaven. In the night vision I saw him at the door of the temple in heaven. He came to me and spoke to me.* He said he could not stop to talk with me because he was in a hurry. The next man I met was Father Smith [the Prophet's father]; he could not talk with me because he was in a hurry. *I met half a dozen brethren who had held high positions on earth*, and none of them could stop to talk with me because they were in a hurry . . . By and by I saw the Prophet again and I got the privilege of asking him a question.
>
> "Now," said I, "I want to know why you are in a hurry . . ."
>
> Joseph Said: "I will tell you, Brother Woodruff . . . We are the last dispensation, and so much work has to be done, and we need to be in a hurry in order to accomplish it."[20]

Therefore, President Woodruff saw the spirit bodies of the Prophet Joseph Smith, his brother Hyrum, their mortal father, and half a dozen brethren who had held high positions on earth. They looked exactly like they did in mortality. The Prophet Joseph Smith personally spoke to President Woodruff, and the voice of the Prophet was the same as it was in mortality. It is reasonable to believe that their spirit bodies had color or pigmentation, the same as when they were mortals. Thus, this narrative adequately explains that a *"spirit continues to exist in another realm called 'the spirit world' and still maintains its form and shape and identity."*[21]

When a member of the Quorum of the Twelve Apostles, President Woodruff said,

> But during my travels in the southern country last winter I had *many interviews with President [Brigham] Young, and with Heber C. Kimball, and Geo. A. Smith, and Jedediah M. Grant, and many others who are dead* . . .
>
> I saw Brother Brigham and Brother Heber ride in carriage ahead of the carriage in which I rode when I was on my way to attend conference; and they were dressed in the most priestly robes. When we arrived at our destination I asked Prest. Young if he would preach to us. He said, "No, I have finished my testimony in the flesh. I shall not talk to this people any more. But (said he) I have come to see you; I have come to watch over you, and to see what the people are doing. Then (said he) I want you to teach the people—and I want you to follow this counsel yourself—that they must labor and so live as to obtain the Holy Spirit . . ."
>
> And I believe myself that these men who have died and gone into the spirit world had this mission left with them, that is, a certain portion of them, to watch over the latter-day Saints.[22]

From this description, President Woodruff was able to see President Brigham Young, Heber C. Kimball, George A. Smith, Jedediah M. Grant, and many others who are dead. President Woodruff was once able to see how President Young and Heber C. Kimball were dressed. Each of these deceased brethren looked exactly like they did in mortality. President Brigham Young personally spoke to President Woodruff, and the voice of President Young was the same as it was in mortality. It is reasonable to believe their spirit bodies had color or pigmentation, the same as when they were mortals. Thus, this narrative adequately explains again that a *"spirit continues to exist in another realm called 'the spirit world' and still maintains its form and shape and identity."*[23]

## Spirit and Physical Deformities

Regarding physical deformities and disfigurements manifested in mortality and their relationship to the spirit housed in the mortal tabernacle, Elder Orson Pratt provides this explanation:

> We, as Latter-day Saints, believe that the spirits that occupy these tabernacles have form and likeness similar to the human tabernacle. *Of course there may be deformities existing in connection with the outward tabernacle which do not exist in connection with the spirit that inhabits it. These tabernacles become deformed by accident in various ways, sometimes at birth, but this may not altogether or in any degree deform the spirits that dwell within them,* therefore, we believe that the spirits which occupy the bodies of the human family are more or less in the resemblance of the tabernacles.[24]

In addition to this statement, these informative words were spoken by Elder James E. Talmage:

> We know but little of things beyond the sphere upon which we live except as information has been revealed by a power superior to that of earth, and by an intelligence above that of man. Notwithstanding the assumption that man is the culmination of an evolutionary development from a lower order of beings, *we know that the body of man today is in the very form and fashion of his spirit, except indeed for disfigurements and deformities.* The perfect body is the counterpart of the perfect spirit and the two are the constituent entities of the soul.[25]

From these statements, it can be determined that physical

31

deformities have no real correlation between the spirit and the mortal body. To support this teaching—especially as it pertains to the resurrection of the body and the spirit—the scripture reveals this knowledge:

> *The spirit and the body shall be reunited again in its perfect form; both limb and joint shall be restored to its proper frame* . . .
>
> Now, this restoration shall come to all, both old and young . . . both male and female . . . and even there shall not so much as a hair of their heads be lost; *but everything shall be restored to its perfect frame.* (Alma 11:43–44; emphasis added)

## Conclusion

Other than physical deformities, the mortal body is in the express image of the spirit housed in it. Therefore, if we could see our spirit body standing by our mortal body, we would see that they have the same look, are the same size, have the same shape, and have the same identity. In complete harmony with this teaching, the Lord has revealed this great truth, "*The spirit of man in the likeness of his person* (D&C 77:2; emphasis added).

## Notes

1. Harold B. Lee, "Be Loyal to the Royal Within You," Brigham Young University stake conference address, p. 6, October 20, 1957; emphasis added.
2. Orson Pratt, "Figure and Magnitude of Spirits," *The Seer*, Vol. 1, No. 3 (Washington, DC Edition, March, 1853), 36. Said Elder Pratt: "Spirits, therefore, must be composed of substances, highly elastic in their nature, that is, they have the power to resume their former dimensions."

3. Harold B. Lee, address given at the 52nd Annual Primary Conference of The Church of Jesus Christ of Latter-day Saints, pp. 5–6, April 3, 1958; emphasis added.

4. Eldred G. Smith, in Conference Report, April 5, 1963, 18; emphasis added.

5. Eldred G. Smith, in Conference Report, October 2, 1964, 10; emphasis added.

6. Orson Pratt, *Journal of Discourses*, 26 vols. (London: Latter-day Saints Book Depot, 1854–86), 2:341; emphasis added.

7. Abraham 3:26.

8. Pratt, *Journal of Discourses*, 19:287; emphasis added.

9. Pratt, *Journal of Discourses*, 2:239; emphasis added.

10. James E. Talmage, "The Earth and Man." Address given August 9, 1931; *The Millennial Star*, December 31, 1931, 93:853–54; emphasis added.

11. Pratt, *Journal of Discourses*, 19:287.

12. Joseph F. Smith, *Gospel Doctrine: Selections from the Sermons and Writings of Joseph F. Smith* (Salt Lake City: Deseret Book, 1971), 455; emphasis added.

13. While blessing and naming an infant son of Reynolds Cahoon, the Prophet Joseph Smith gave the boy the name of Mahonri Moriancumer. Turning to Elder Cahoon, he said, "The name I have given your son is the name of the Brother of Jared; the Lord has just shown (or revealed) it to me" (*Improvement Era*, 8:704–705). This account is written in Bruce R. McConkie's *Mormon Doctrine*, 2nd ed. (Salt Lake City: Bookcraft, 1966), 463.

14. B. H. Roberts, *Young Woman's Journal* 27, September 1916, 524–30; emphasis added.

15. Ibid.

16. Ibid.

17. James E. Talmage, in Conference Report, April 8, 1928, 96; emphasis added.

18. Hartman Rector Jr., in Conference Report, October 3, 1970, 73; emphasis added.

19. Matthias F. Cowley, *Wilford Woodruff, History of His Life and Labors* (Salt Lake City: Bookcraft, 1978), 93; emphasis added.

20. Wilford Woodruff, *The Discourses of Wilford Woodruff*, selected by G. Homer Durham (Salt Lake City: Bookcraft, 1969), 288–89.
21. Rector, in Conference Report.
22. Wilford Woodruff, October 10, 1880; *Journal of Discourses*, 21:318; emphasis added.
23. Rector, in Conference Report, 73.
24. Pratt; *Journal of Discourses*, 15:242–43; emphasis added.
25. Talmage, "The Earth and Man," *The Millennial Star*, 93:853–54; emphasis added. The word *today* has been modernized.

## CHAPTER 4

# DEFINING DEATH

## REAL EMOTIONS EVOKED BY DEATH

Repeatedly death comes as unexpectedly as the first winter's frost. It is perceived as an enemy who suddenly appears without warning. Evoking pangs of sorrow and emptiness for those left behind, the loss and hurt are real. Only its intensity varies between individuals and family members.

Many times death silences the laughter of little children. It takes away those who are midway in life's journey, and it comes to the aged. For those individuals who experience great suffering and illness, death comes as an angel of mercy. Yet, even when the elderly or infirm have found merciful relief, their loved ones are rarely ready to let them depart. Death eventually comes to all mankind. It is no respecter of age, gender, or race. It is appropriately stated that all people are only one breath away from death.

It is natural that we mourn for those loved and taken by the heavy hand of death. One of the deepest expressions of pure love is mourning. Knowing that we would experience the loss of loved ones, the Lord revealed this knowledge to the Prophet Joseph Smith: "Thou shalt live together in love, insomuch that thou shalt weep for the loss of them that die" (D&C 42:45).

Though death evokes a variety of emotions, it should be

viewed as a natural consequence of mortality. Eternal perspective provides peace "which passeth all understanding" (Philippians 4:7). It is true that life does not begin with mortal birth, nor does it end with physical death. In the premortal life, we shouted for joy at the privilege of coming to earth and gaining a physical body (see Job 38:7). We knew then that the Father's plan called for the creation of this earth, where we could live as mortals, receive physical bodies made from the dust of the earth, and undergo the tests and trials that would transpire in mortality. To place death in its proper perspective, a brief explanation of the Father's plan of salvation will be given.

## PLAN OF SALVATION

Prior to our mortal birth, we lived in a place called the premortal existence. We dwelled as spirit children with our Heavenly Father. God the Father ordained and established the plan of salvation to enable us to advance and progress from our spirit state to a state of absolute joy and happiness (exaltation), which He possesses. In this spirit realm, we anticipated the day of coming to earth and obtaining a physical body. We knew that our Father's great plan of progression called for a birth that would provide a mortal tabernacle for our eternal spirits, and for a death that would free our spirits from the trials and weaknesses of mortality.

It is revealed that "this life [is] a probationary state; a time to prepare to meet God" (Alma 12:24). It is an estate in which we are tested physically, mentally, morally, and spiritually. We are subject to trials, disease, and decay. We are called upon to choose between the revealed word of God, given to us through the scriptures and by the Lord's chosen leaders, or the theology of man and theories of science.

Now, what of death?

In the Book of Mormon it is written that "death hath passed upon all men, to fulfil the merciful plan of the great Creator"

(2 Nephi 9:6). The writer of Ecclesiastes said: "To every thing there is a season, and a time to every purpose under the heaven: A time to be born, and a time to die" (Ecclesiastes 3:1–2; see also Alma 12:27). Our limited understanding would be enlarged if we could see the reunion on the other side of the veil, when death allows individuals to be reunited with friends and loved ones in the spirit world who previously departed mortal life through the same portal of death.

It is important to emphasize that we do not seek death, though it is part of the merciful plan of God the Father. We rejoice in life and desire to live as long as we can in mortality. Yet, when death eventually comes, it can be peaceful and sweet. To help our understanding of these verities, we now turn our attention to informative and uplifting statements made by General Authorities and information revealed in the scriptures.

## PHYSICAL DEATH

When Adam and Eve partook of the forbidden fruit, a dramatic but painless change occurred—blood began to flow in their veins; therefore, they became mortal beings.[1] Accordingly, the bodies of our first parents were changed to permit them to have offspring and fulfill the purposes in the creation of this earth (see D&C 29:40–43; Moses 5:10–11; 2 Nephi 2:19–25). By a divine law put in force, death and mortality entered the world. Concerning this doctrine, Alma provided this explanation:

> Now we see that Adam did fall by the partaking of the forbidden fruit, according to the word of God; and thus we see, that by his fall, all mankind became a lost and fallen people.
>
> And now behold, I say unto you that if it had been possible for Adam to have partaken of the fruit of the tree of life at that time, there would have been no death, and the word would have been void, making God a liar, for he said: If thou eat thou shalt surely die.
>
> And we see that death comes upon mankind, yea, the death

which has been spoken of by Amulek, which is the temporal death; nevertheless there was a space granted unto man in which he might repent; therefore this life became a probationary state; a time to prepare to meet God; a time to prepare for that endless state which has been spoken of by us, which is after the resurrection of the dead. (Alma 12:22–24)

Two kinds of death are referred to in the scriptures. *One is spiritual death,* when an individual is cast out of the presence of the Lord, to die pertaining to righteousness and the things of the Spirit. *The other is the physical death, which is caused by the separation of the spirit from the mortal body.* As recorded in the New Testament, it is aptly written that "the body without the spirit is dead" (James 2:26).

Regarding physical death, the scriptures generally refer to it as the *natural* or *temporal* death. In addition to the scriptures recorded in the Book of Mormon, Alma 11:42; 12:16, 24; 42:8; and Mormon 9:13, the Prophet Joseph Smith received this revelation in the presence of six elders:

But, behold, I say unto you that I, the Lord God, gave unto Adam and unto his seed, that they should not die *as to the temporal death*, until I, the Lord God, should send forth angels to declare unto them repentance and redemption, through faith on the name of mine Only Begotten Son.

And thus did I, the Lord God, appoint unto man the days of his probation—that *by his natural death* he might be raised in immortality unto eternal life, even a many as would believe. (D&C 29:42–43; emphasis added)

Concerning the natural or temporal death, President Brigham Young made these informative remarks:

In many places in the scriptures, the separation of the body and spirit is called death; but that is not death in the strict sense of the term; *that is only a change.*[2]

Using logic, he gave the follow illustration:

We are naturally inclined to cling to our mother earth; our bodies love to live here, to see, to hear, to breathe, and to enjoy themselves, because we are of the earth, earthy. But probably, in most cases, the change from mortal to immortality is no greater, comparatively speaking, than when a child emerges into this world. We shall suffer no more in putting off this flesh and leaving the spirit houseless than the child, in its capacity, does in its first efforts to breathe the breath of this mortal life.[3]

Explaining where the spirit goes after death occurs, President Young revealed this knowledge:

After the spirit leaves the body, it remains without a tabernacle in the spirit world until the Lord, by his law that he has ordained, brings to pass the resurrection of the dead . . .

*Spirits, when they leave their bodies, do not dwell with the Father and the Son, but live in the spirit world, where there are places prepared for them.* Those who do honor to their tabernacles, who love and believe in the Lord Jesus Christ, must put off this mortality, or they cannot put on immortality. This body must be changed, else it cannot be prepared to dwell in the glory of the Father.[4]

President Heber C. Kimball, then First Counselor in the First Presidency, gave this description:

We say the dead have departed this life as though they had departed to some other life. This, however, is not so; *dying is like going from one room to another*, or from one part of the earth to another, the *life still exists though the body decays*, but the life which dwelt in it is indestructible.[5]

At the funeral of Sister Elizabeth H. Cannon, President Wilford Woodruff, then President of the Quorum of the Twelve Apostles, expressed that death was a birth into the spirit world:

On such occasions when mourning the loss of our departed friends, I cannot help but think that *in every death there is a birth*: the spirit leaves the body dead to us, and passes to the other side of the [veil] alive to that great and noble company that are also working for the accomplishment of the purposes of God, in the redemption and salvation of a fallen world.[6]

At the same funeral service, President John Taylor gave this definition of death:

> The present is only *one stage of our existence.* We existed before we came here; we exist here for a time, and when we depart from this mortal life we shall have a spiritual existence . . . without the body, and then again with the body [at the Resurrection].[7]

In one of his many sermons, Elder Franklin D. Richards, a member of the Quorum of the Twelve Apostles, said this of death:

> Latter-day Saints who live their religion having a testimony of Jesus, have no fear of death. *We look at it as but a stepping stone from one apartment of God's great creation to another.* When we leave our kindred here, we will be united with a great number there; and some of our very dearest kindred are there waiting for us: Wives, parents, fathers and mothers, brothers and sisters, children of all ages await our presence there.[8]

While speaking to members of The Church of Jesus Christ of Latter-day Saints, President George Q. Cannon, then First Counselor in the First Presidency, asked: "What is death?" Answering, he expressed this confident belief:

> It is only a change from this condition [in mortality] into a better one. We of all people should be the least afraid of death, because God has made the greatest of promises to us. If we are valiant in His cause, He will reward us and crown us with glory; for He loves valor.[9]

In harmony with the teaching of President Cannon, Elder Orson F. Whitney, a member of the Quorum of the Twelve Apostles, expressed this belief:

"O death! where is thy sting? O grave! where is thy victory?"

The Comforter teaches us of the past, the present, and the future, and this knowledge, with the peace which the Gospel brings through the outpourings of the Holy Spirit, takes from death its bitterness, and triumphs over the grave. There is no death for the righteous—*change, but not death*, for the children of the Light.[10]

Several years later, Elder Whitney provided another explanation:

It never crushes me when a dear one departs; for I have learned some things about death that prevent me from taking gloomy and hopeless views of the subject. "When I was a child I spake as a child, I understood as a child, I thought as a child; but when I became a man, I put away childish things."

I used to think that when the body was lowered into the ground, that was the end of all. That was what death meant to me then. But I have learned better . . .

Everything around us, animate or inanimate, obeys a great natural law and returns to the place from which it came. We ourselves are subject to that law. It is just as natural to go out of this life as it is to come into it; *and what we call death is the doorway out of the world*, as birth is the doorway into it.[11]

## CONCLUSION

From these informative and uplifting statements, the natural or temporal death has appropriately been defined by the Lord's chosen servants as follows:

(1) Spirits, when they leave their bodies, live in the spirit world, where there are places prepared for them.

(2) Dying is like going from one room to another; life still exists though the body decays.

(3) A birth into the spirit world.

(4) One stage of our existence.

(5) A stepping stone from one apartment of God's creation to another.

(6) A change from this condition to a better one.

(7) A doorway out of this world.

---

## Notes

1. It is written, "The life of the flesh is in the blood" (Leviticus 17:11). See also Matthew 16:17 and 1 Corinthians 15:50; Joseph Fielding Smith, *Man: His Origin and Destiny* (Salt Lake City: Deseret Book, 1954), 362, 364; Joseph Fielding Smith, *Doctrines of Salvation*, compiled by Bruce R. McConkie, 3 vols. (Salt Lake City: Bookcraft, 1954–56) 1:77.

   Using logic, all mortals who are born on earth have blood flowing in their veins. Excepting rare cases, there is no pain with blood flowing throughout the mortal body; it is a natural function. Accordingly, when blood began to flow in their veins, the same natural and painless function would have applied to Adam and Eve.

2. Brigham Young, *Journal of Discourses*, 26 vols. (London: Latter-day Saints Book Depot, 1854–86), 8:28; emphasis added. The word *scriptures* has been modernized.

3. Ibid., 8:28.

4. Ibid., 8:28–29; emphasis added. Spelling of the words *spirit world* and *honor* have been modernized. Concerning the spirit world, see also *Journal of Discourses*, 3:369 and 6:294; emphasis added.

5. Heber C. Kimball, *Journal of Discourses*, 10:100; emphasis added.

6. Wilford Woodruff, funeral services of Sister Elizabeth H. Cannon, January 29, 1882; *Journal of Discourses*, 22:348; emphasis added.

7. John Taylor, funeral services of Sister Elizabeth H. Cannon, January 29, 1882; *Journal of Discourses*, 22:354; emphasis added.

8. Franklin D. Richards, *Collected Discourses*, 2nd ed., compiled and edited by Brian H. Stuy (Scarborough, Canada: BHS Publishing, 1886–89), 1:4; emphasis added, punctuation modernized.

9. George Q. Cannon, *Deseret News Weekly*, No. 22, May 15, 1897, 54:676; emphasis added.

10. Orson F. Whitney, funeral address, April 1910; *Young Woman's Journal* (Salt Lake City, June 1910), 21:300; emphasis added.

11. Orson F. Whitney, *Young Woman's Journal* (Salt Lake City, April 1928), 39:204; emphasis added.

CHAPTER 5

# THE SEPARATION OF SPIRIT AND BODY

## INFORMATIVE STATEMENTS

When physical death occurs, a spirit that is temporarily housed in a mortal body departs and goes into a place called the spirit world.

This teaching is verified by the declarative words spoken by Alma, as recorded in the Book of Mormon:

> Behold, it has been made known unto me by an angel, that the spirits of all men [mankind], as soon as they are departed from this mortal body, yea, the spirits of all men, whether they be good or evil, are taken home to that God who gave them life.
>
> "The spirits of those who are righteous are received into a state of happiness, *which is called paradise*, a state of rest, a state of peace. (Alma 40:11–12; emphasis added)

Speaking as a "linguist," the Prophet Joseph Smith explained that "Hades, the Greek, or Sheol, the Hebrew, these two significations mean a world of spirits. Hades, Sheol, *paradise*, spirits in prison, are all one: *it is a world of spirits.*"[1]

Numerous people have wondered how a spirit leaves its mortal tabernacle and goes into "a world of spirits." President Brigham Young told an interesting story of a spirit leaving its physical body. At a meeting held in the Tabernacle at Salt Lake City,

45

Utah, in 1860, Elder Orson Hyde, a member of the Quorum of the Twelve Apostles, spoke first. He briefly told of an article that was published concerning a Mr. Davis. President Young was the next speaker and provided additional information:

> Brother Hyde . . . referred to a statement made by Andrew Jackson Davis. He placed himself in a clairvoyant state [the power or faculty of discerning objects not present to the senses][2] beside the bed of a sick person and observed the spirit of a lady leave her body. *He saw the spirit ascend from the head of the mortal tenement*—saw it walk out into the open air *in company with another spirit that came to escort her away.* They appeared to him to ascend an inclined plane, and continued to walk away until they were out of his sight.[3]

Expressing his personal belief, President Young said:

> Do you not believe that your spirit will be in existence after it leaves the body? *I care not whether it goes out from the head or from some other portion.*[4]

From these statements, it is evident that both Elder Hyde and President Young were familiar with a published article concerning an experience observed by a Mr. Davis. In addition, both of these leaders felt a need to talk of what Mr. Davis witnessed.

When Elder Orson Hyde briefly spoke of the experience of Mr. Davis, Elder Hyde began with this qualifying statement:

> With regard to the operation of death, I do not know that I will exactly endorse the principle, but I will take up what Andrew Jackson Davis says. *It is rather singular, and I don't think it is very far from the truth.*[5]

## Silver Cord

During his remarks, President Brigham Young said that Mr. Davis observed that after the spirit was fully out of the body, "*he saw as it were an umbilical cord that yet retained the spirit to the body; and that when that was separated, the spirit was free, and the body was consigned to dissolution.*[6] Various people believe this "umbilical cord" is called a *silver cord*. To support their belief, they quote two verses written in the Old Testament:

> *Or ever the silver cord be loosed*, or the golden bowl be broken, or the pitcher be broken at the fountain, or the wheel broken at the cistern.
> *Then shall the dust return to the earth as it was: and the spirit shall return unto God who gave it.* (Ecclesiastes 12:6–7; emphasis added)

In an acknowledged Bible commentary, this statement is written concerning these verses:

> Commentators have differed much as to the interpretation of this passage. It has been taken by many as a description of the gradual failing of one bodily organ after another till death supervenes [follows].[7]

From published statements, individuals have described the "silver cord as being smooth, very long [and] bright, like an elastic cable made of light, about an inch wide . . . and attached to one of several possible locations on the physical body." When death finally occurs, this silver cord is severed and "the spirit body is released from being attached to the physical body." Some believe that this "silver cord is our spirit body's 'lifeline' to our physical body in the same way that our umbilical cord is our 'lifeline' to our mother's body during the birth process."[8]

Some might classify these statements as interesting speculation, not supported in LDS commentary. Whatever one's belief, the statements are presented for informational consideration.

## "MATTERS NOT"

Returning again to the story briefly related by Elder Orson Hyde of what Mr. Davis observed, Elder Hyde concluded his remarks by saying:

If that live image did come out as he represented, that is the part that shall never die; *and whether it [a spirit] passes out in that particular form, matters not*; we know that it does escape and live for ever.[9]

At the conclusion of President Brigham Young's remarks concerning the statements made by Mr. Davis, President Young stated:

*Whether this be true or not, it is as certain that the spirit leaves the body* . . . When it leaves the body, it dwells in the spirit world until the body is raised up by the power of God.[10]

## CONCLUSION

Though Elder Hyde and President Young spoke of a *"rather singular"* experience observed by Mr. Davis, both of these leaders stated that it *"matters not"* how a spirit leaves its mortal tabernacle. All that is revealed, and perhaps all that we need to know at the present time on this intriguing subject is this: *When physical death occurs*—as explained by Alma and the Prophet Joseph Smith—*a spirit that is temporarily housed in a mortal body departs and goes into a place called the spirit world.*[11]

---

## NOTES

1. Joseph Smith, *Teachings of the Prophet Joseph Smith*, selected by Joseph Fielding Smith (Salt Lake City: Deseret Book, 1976), 310.
2. *Merriam-Webster's Collegiate Dictionary*, 10th ed. (Springfield, Massachusetts: Merriam-Webster, 2000), 210.
3. Brigham Young, *Journal of Discourses*, 26 vols. (London: Latter-day Saints Book Depot, 1854–86), 8:30; emphasis added.
4. Ibid.
5. Orson Hyde, *Journal of Discourses*, 8:25; emphasis added.

6. Young, *Journal of Discourses*, 8:30; emphasis added.
7. *A Commentary on The Holy Bible* (commonly referred to as *The One-Volume Bible Commentary*), edited by The Reverend J. R. Dummelow, 31st ed. (New York: The Macmillan Company, 1970), 400.
8. "The NDE [Near-Death Experiences] and the Silver Cord," Internet website (www.near-death.com/experiences/research12.html), Kevin Williams's research conclusions. Accessed November 16, 2010. See also "Silver cord" and "Astral projection" in Wikipedia, the free encyclopedia Internet website (http://en.wikipedia.org/wiki/Silver_cord and http://en.wikipedia.org/wiki/astral_projection). Accessed November 16, 2010.
9. Hyde, *Journal of Discourses*, 8:26; emphasis added.
10. Young, *Journal of Discourses*, 8:30; emphasis added.
11. Alma 40:11–14; Smith, *Teachings of the Prophet Joseph Smith*, 310.

CHAPTER 6

# DEATHS OF INFANTS
# AND CHILDREN

## CHILDREN IN HEAVEN

From the days of Adam to the present, a myriad of infants and children have been taken from loved ones by the hand of death. Either silently or verbally this searching question has been asked, "Why?" To help answer, we turn to the Prophet Joseph Smith for explanation.

> We have again the warning voice sounded in our midst, which shows the uncertainty of human life; and in my leisure moments I have meditated upon the subject, and asked the question, why it is that infants, innocent children, are taken away from us, especially those that seem to be the most intelligent and interesting. The strongest reasons that present themselves to my mind are these: This world is a very wicked world; and it . . . grows more wicked and corrupt.[1]

Then, he spoke these assuring and comforting words:

> The Lord takes many away even in infancy, that they may escape the envy of man, and the sorrows and evils of this present world; they were too pure, too lovely, to live on earth; therefore, if rightly considered, instead of mourning we have reason to rejoice as they are delivered from evil, and we shall soon have them again.[2]

Later in his discourse, he made this observation:

> The only difference between the old and young dying is, one lives longer in heaven and eternal light and glory than the other, and is freed a little sooner from this miserable wicked world. Notwithstanding all this glory, we for a moment lose sight of it, and mourn the loss, but we do not mourn as those without hope.[3]

Though it is natural and proper that we mourn for infants and children who are taken away by the Lord, these inspired words spoken by the Prophet Joseph Smith provide insight and solace to parents and loved ones. Knowing that these individuals were too pure, too lovely, to live on earth brings great assurance and comfort. It is important to reemphasize that in the premortal life, we shouted for joy at the privilege of coming to earth and gaining a physical body (see Job 38:7). These tiny souls taken by the Lord—regardless of gender or race—have fulfilled this important mission.

## Remarks of President Wilford Woodruff

Concerning infants and children who die, President Wilford Woodruff, then a member of the Quorum of the Twelve Apostles, expressed this thought:

> The question may arise with me and with you—"Why has the Lord taken away my children?"[4]

Answering, he honestly replied:

> But that is not for me to tell, *because I do not know*; it is in the hands of the Lord, and it has been so from the creation of the world all the way down.[5]

President Woodruff then shared the following belief:

> Children are taken away in their infancy, and they go to the spirit world. They come here [to earth] and fulfil the object of their coming, that is, they tabernacle in the

flesh . . . they obtain a body, or tabernacle, and that tabernacle will be preserved for them, and in the morning of the resurrection the spirits and bodies will be reunited . . . Our children will be restored to us as they are laid down if we, their parents, keep the faith and prove ourselves worthy to obtain eternal life; and if we do not so prove ourselves our children will still be preserved, and will inherit celestial glory. This is my view in regard to all infants who die, whether they are born to a Jew or Gentile, righteous or wicked. They come from their eternal father and their eternal mother unto whom they were born in the eternal world, and they will be restored to their eternal parentage; and all parents [on earth] who have received children here according to the order of God . . . no matter in what age they may have lived, will claim those children in the morning of the resurrection, and they will be given unto them and they will grace their family organizations in the celestial world.[6]

In harmony with the teachings of President Woodruff, Elder LeGrand Richards, also a member of the Quorum of the Twelve Apostles, spoke these heartfelt words:

There are those of us who have laid away our little ones in the grave, and we had that responsibility. A little daughter was born to us over in Holland while I was president of the mission there, and we kept her until she was three and a half years old . . . Sometimes I have thought that probably some of these choice spirits did not need the experience here in mortality like other children, and that is why the Lord has seen fit to call them home.[7]

## EXALTATION OF CHILDREN

The Lord has revealed that there are three kingdoms of glory into which resurrected beings will be saved. They are the celestial, the terrestrial, and the telestial (see D&C 76). The highest of these kingdoms of glory is the celestial kingdom. "In the celestial glory there are three heavens or degrees" (D&C 131:1). The Lord has revealed that the reward for individuals who are righteous will be the highest glory in the celestial kingdom (see D&C 131 and 132).

Because of the great atoning sacrifice of our Savior, infants and children are alive in Christ. "Little children are redeemed from the foundation of the world through mine Only Begotten," said the Lord, "Wherefore, they cannot sin, for power is not given unto Satan to tempt little children, until they begin to become accountable before me" (D&C 29:46–47).

In writing to his son Moroni, Mormon spoke these authoritative words, "little children need no repentance, neither baptism" (Moroni 8:11). Later in his epistle, he declared: "And he that saith that little children need baptism denieth the mercies of Christ, and setteth at naught the atonement of him and the power of his redemption" (Moroni 8:20).

In a vision of the celestial kingdom, the Prophet Joseph Smith declared: "And I also beheld that all children who die before they arrive at the years of accountability, are saved in the celestial kingdom of heaven."[8]

Regarding the Prophet's statement, President Joseph Fielding Smith, then a member of the Quorum of the Twelve Apostles, wrote these clarifying words: "Little children who die before they reach the years of accountability will automatically inherit the celestial kingdom, but not the exaltation in that kingdom *until* they have complied with all the requirements of exaltation. For instance:

> The crowning glory is marriage and this ordinance would have to be performed in their behalf *before* they could inherit the fulness of that kingdom.[9] (See also D&C 131 and 132.)

He then wrote these assuring words:

> Children who die in childhood will not be deprived of any blessing. When they grow, after the resurrection, to the full maturity of the spirit, *they will be entitled to all the blessings which they would have been entitled to had they been privileged to tarry*

*here* [on earth] *and receive them* [as deemed worthy]. The Lord has arranged for that, so that justice will be given to every soul.[10]

## REMARKS OF PRESIDENT JOSEPH F. SMITH

At the funeral of Daniel Wells Grant, child of Elder Heber J. Grant (who later became President of the Church) and Emily Wells Grant, President Joseph F. Smith, then Second Counselor in the First Presidency, spoke these comforting words:

> If we have received the testimony of the spirit of truth in our souls we know that all is well with our little children who pass away, that we could not, if we would, better their condition.
>
> But, with little children who are taken away in infancy and innocence before they have reached the years of accountability, and are not capable of committing sin, the gospel reveals to us the fact that they are redeemed, and Satan has no power over them. Neither has death any power over them. They are redeemed by the blood of Christ, and they are saved just as surely as death has come into the world through the fall of our first parents . . . To my mind this is a consolation and a glorious truth that my soul delights in. I am grateful to my heavenly Father that he has revealed it unto me, for it affords a consolation that nothing else can give, and it brings a joy to my spirit that nothing can take away.[11]

Directing his remarks to those individuals who have had infants and children pass away, he wrote these encouraging words:

> Under these circumstances, our beloved friends who are now deprived of their little one, have great cause for joy and rejoicing, even in the midst of deep sorrow that they feel at the loss of their little one for a time. They know he is all right; they have the assurance that their little one has passed away without sin. Such children are in the bosom of the Father. They will inherit their glory and their exaltation, and they will not be deprived of the blessings that belong to them . . . They will lose nothing by being taken away from us in this way.[12]

Speaking for himself, he testified:

This is a consolation to me. Joseph Smith, the prophet, was the promulgator under God of these principles. He was in touch with the heavens. God revealed himself unto him, and made known unto him the principles that lie before us, and which are comprised in the everlasting gospel.[13]

President Smith then provided this explanation:

Joseph Smith declared that the mother who laid down her little child, being deprived of the privilege, the joy, and the satisfaction of bringing it up to manhood or womanhood in this world, would, after the resurrection, have all the joy, satisfaction and pleasure, and even more than it would have been possible to have had in mortality, in seeing her child grow to the full measure of the stature of its spirit.[14]

Speaking personally, he sincerely stated:

With these thoughts in my mind, I take consolation in the fact that I shall meet my children who have passed behind the veil; I have lost a number, and I have felt all that a parent can feel, I think, in the loss of my children. I have felt it keenly, for I love children, and I am particularly fond of the little ones, but I feel thankful to God for the knowledge of these principles, because now I have every confidence in his word and in his promise that I will possess in the future all that belongs to me, and my joy will be full. I will not be deprived of any privilege or any blessing that I am worthy of and that may be properly entrusted to me.[15]

Directing his remarks to Elder and Sister Grant, he spoke these assuring words:

I know that Brother Heber and his companion, if they are faithful to the light they possess and to the covenants that they have entered into before the Lord, will just as assuredly inherit the joy and the possession and the glory of this little one that has now departed, as that they see its little form lying here before them this moment. Everyone who has the spirit of truth in his soul must feel this to be true.[16]

# DEATH OF PRESIDENT SMITH'S GRANDSON

President Joseph F. Smith was no stranger to the death of loved ones. He was five when his father, Hyrum Smith, was killed with the Prophet Joseph Smith in Carthage Jail. His beloved mother, Mary, died when he was thirteen. His wife Sarah Richards Smith died in 1915; later that year his daughter Zina Smith Greenwell passed away. Thirteen of his forty-four children died, many in their childhood.[17]

Responding to a letter written by a relative, President Smith wrote these heart-felt, yet testifying words about a grandson who had passed away:

> Bee Hive House, Salt Lake City, Jan. 11th 1906.
>
> Elder Willard S. Smith . . .
>
> My own Beloved Son Willard: . . .
>
> In your letter of the 12th you mention the sad news you rec'd of the death of Mamie's darling little boy [Mamie is a daughter of President Smith and the little boy a grandson].
>
> This was one of the [saddest] scenes of my life. If it had been Mamie herself I could have stood it almost as well. To see my Mamie suffer the grief of her irreparable loss, was worse, if possible, to bear than the actual death of that sweet little babe. We all loved him so, and all were so happy to know that Mamie had him, that to lose him, and to witness her disappointment and grief was to me heartrending. But in the sure knowledge that "he's not dead, but sleepeth," and that he is ours, and we will have him again if we are faithful, we find comfort and hope, and thank the Lord for his brief visit on earth.[18]

## NATURAL PRINCIPLES

When an infant or child dies—regardless of the age or the stage of its development—there is a physical cause for his or her death. In an address to members of The Church of Jesus Christ of Latter-day Saints, President Charles W. Penrose, then Second Counselor in the First Presidency, spoke the following words about natural principles:

> We reflect upon our mortal career, and see the infant, a little infant, so innocent of any evil when we see the young child, or a young man or young woman, or middle-aged person in the vigor of physical strength and maturity, *when we see them depart, we say, "Well, how is that, why is that?"*[19]

Using logic, he gave this explanation:

> Why, brethren and sisters, it is just as natural as any result that comes from a cause. There are causes which bring the effects of premature decay or death.[20]

Giving reasons for the death of individuals, President Penrose shared this insight:

> Don't think for a moment there is some one sent here with vengeance to smite down the infant or the young child or the middle-age man or even the old man when he comes to the time that he has to depart, that somebody comes and takes him away. Don't think that. There are *natural principles* that lie behind life and death, and there will be in the resurrection. *Sometimes evils, faults, exist in individuals and they lay the foundation in themselves for premature departure; sometimes it is the fault of parents; sometimes it comes from a remote ancestry, but there are causes for all the afflictions we find here in the earth, and they act on natural principles.*[21]

Thus, infants and children—as with all mankind—experience premature death because of various reasons. Accordingly, there are natural causes and principles that lie behind life and death. Prior to being born in mortality, spirit children of our Heavenly Father have reached adulthood. Regarding the spirit and how it affects the growth and size of the physical body it is temporarily housed in, we rely upon the wisdom of Elder Orson Pratt:

> The tabernacles of both animals and vegetables continue to grow or increase in size, until they attain to the original magnitude of their respective spirits, after which the growth ceases. When the spirit first takes possession of the vegetable or animal seed or embryo, it contracts itself into a bulk of the same dimension as the seed or tabernacle into which it enters: . . . Spirits, therefore, must be composed of substances, highly elastic in their nature, that is, they have the power to resume their former dimensions, as additional matter is secreted for the enlargement of their tabernacles. It is this expanding force, exerted by the spirit, which gradually develops the tabernacle as the necessary materials are supplied.[22]

From this explanation it is apparent that the spirit is quite elastic. The spirit leaves the premortal estate as a full grown entity, and upon entering the seed or physical body, it "contracts" to the size of the person, animal, or plant. Then, through a period of mortal months or years, attains to the physical height the spirit had reached in the premortal life.

## Children Who Die Can Be Seen as Children

Spirits of departed infants and children have appeared in the form of an infant or child at times to those individuals who would be able to identify them in that manner. President Jedediah M. Grant, then Second Counselor in the First Presidency, was able to see his daughter as a tiny baby while his spirit was in the spirit world. At the funeral services of President Grant, President Heber C. Kimball, then First Counselor in the First Presidency, revealed this information:

He saw his wife; she was the first person that came to him. He saw many that he knew, but did not have conversation with any except his wife Caroline. She came to him, and he said that she looked beautiful and had their little child, that died on the Plains, in her arms, and said, "Mr. Grant, here is little Margaret; you know that the wolves ate her up, but it did not hurt her; here she is all right."[23]

In harmony with the statement of President Kimball, President Joseph F. Smith declared:

The spirits of our children are immortal before they come to us, and their spirits, *after bodily death, are like they were before they came.* They are as they would have appeared if they had lived in the flesh, to grow to maturity, or to develop their physical bodies to the full stature of their spirits.[24]

In regard to recognizing deceased children, he then provides this teaching:

If you see one of your children that has passed away it may appear to you in the form in which you would recognize it, the form of childhood.[25]

In reference to a deceased child coming as a messenger from the presence of God, he provided this explanation:

But if it *came to you as a messenger bearing some important truth,* it would perhaps come as the spirit of Bishop Edward Hunter's son (who died when a little child) came to him, *in the stature of full-grown manhood,* and revealed himself to his father, and said: "I am your son."[26]

Providing additional information, President Smith continued:

Bishop Hunter did not understand it. He went to my father [Hyrum Smith, the Prophet Joseph Smith's brother] and said: "Hyrum, what does that mean? I buried my son when he was only a little boy, but he has come to me as a full-grown man—a noble, glorious, young man, and declared himself [as] my son.

What does it mean?"

Father (Hyrum Smith, the patriarch) told him that the Spirit of Jesus Christ was full-grown before he was born into the world; and so *our children were full-grown and possessed their full stature in the spirit, before they entered mortality, the same stature that they will posses after they have passed away from mortality, and as they will also appear after the resurrection, when they shall have completed their mission.*[27]

Likewise, Elder Melvin J. Ballard, a member of the Quorum of the Twelve Apostles, related an appearance of his deceased son and gave this description: "I lost a son six years of age, and I *saw him a man in the spirit world after his death*."[28]

From these statements, it is evident that as soon as an infant or child dies, it becomes a full-grown spirit in the spirit world. However, the spirits of these little ones have appeared in the form of an infant or child at times to those individuals who would be able to identify them in that manner.

## STATUS OF CHILDREN IN THE RESURRECTION

President Joseph F. Smith taught the status of children in the Resurrection:

[The Prophet] Joseph Smith taught the doctrine that the infant child that was laid away in death would come up in the resurrection as a child; and, pointing to the mother of a lifeless child, he said to her: "*You will have the joy, the pleasure, and satisfaction of nurturing this child, after its resurrection, until it reaches the full stature of its spirit.*" There is restitution, there is growth, there is development, after the resurrection from death. I love this truth. It speaks volumes of happiness, of joy and gratitude to my soul. Thank the Lord he has revealed these principles to us.[29]

President Smith explained that, "the mother of that little girl that Joseph Smith, the Prophet, was speaking about" was his "aunt, the wife of my uncle, Don Carlos Smith."[30]

President Smith also said that,

> One day I was conversing with a brother-in-law of mine,
> Lorin Walker, who married my oldest sister. In the course of the
> conversation he happened to mention that he was present at the
> funeral of my cousin Sophronia, and that he heard the Prophet
> Joseph Smith declare the very words that Aunt Agnes had told
> me.[31]

Later, President Smith was "in conversation with Sister M.
Isabella Horne. She began to relate to me the circumstances of
her being present at the funeral that I refer to." Sister Horne said
that her "husband was there." President Smith then wrote,

> So I have the testimony in affidavit form of Brother and
> Sister Horne, in addition to the testimony of my aunt, and
> the testimony of my brother-in-law, in relation to the Prophet
> Joseph's remarks at that funeral.[32]

Continuing, he happily declared:

> Just a little while later, to my joy and satisfaction, the first man
> I ever heard mention it in public was [Elder] Franklin D. [Dewey]
> Richards [a member of the Quorum of the Twelve Apostles];
> and when he spoke of it, I felt it in my soul: the truth has come
> out . . . Presidents Woodruff and Cannon [of the First Presidency]
> approved of the doctrine and after that I preached it.[33]

Accordingly, the Prophet "Joseph Smith taught the doctrine
that the infant child that was laid away in death would come up
in the resurrection as a child; and that its mother—it must be
added: If worthy—'will have the joy, the pleasure, and satisfaction of nurturing this child, after its resurrection, until it reaches
the full stature of its spirit.'"[34]

This teaching is clarified and supported by the teaching of
President Joseph Fielding Smith, then a member of the Quorum
of the Twelve Apostles:

When a baby dies, it goes back into the spirit world, and the spirit assumes its natural form as an adult, for we were all adults before we were born.

When a child is raised in the resurrection, the spirit will enter the body and the body will be the same size as it was when the child died. It will then *grow after the resurrection* to full maturity to conform to the size of the spirit.

If parents are righteous, they will have their children after the resurrection. Little children who die, whose parents are not worthy of an exaltation, will be *adopted* into the families of those who are worthy.[35]

In a personal letter, President Smith wrote these comforting words:

> *Satan cannot tempt little children in this life, nor in the spirit world, nor after their resurrection.* Little children who die before reaching the years of accountability will not be tempted; those born during the millennium, when Satan is bound and cannot tempt them, "shall grow up without sin unto salvation."[36]

## CONCLUSION

These inspired teachings adequately explain that infants and children who have not reached the years of accountability are saved in the celestial kingdom. After the Resurrection, when children grow to the full maturity of their individual spirit, they will be entitled to all the blessings of the gospel. The Lord has arranged for that. Faithful parents will have the joy, the satisfaction, and the pleasure of seeing their child grow to the full measure of the stature of his or her spirit. It is important to emphasize that Satan cannot tempt little children in this life, nor in the spirit world, nor after their resurrection. Therefore, these precious infants and children are saved through the Atonement of our Savior, Jesus Christ.

## Notes

1. Joseph Smith, "The Prophet's Sermon on Life and Death; the Resurrection and the Salvation of Children," *Teachings of the Prophet Joseph Smith*, selected by Joseph Fielding Smith (Salt Lake City: Deseret Book, 1976), 196; emphasis added. See also *History of The Church of Jesus Christ of Latter-day Saints*, 7 vols., edited by B. H. Roberts (Salt Lake City: Deseret Book, 1976), 4:553–54; originally given on Sunday, March 20, 1842, Nauvoo, Illinois, and reported by Wilford Woodruff; emphasis added.

2. Ibid., 196–97

3. Ibid., 197.

4. Wilford Woodruff, as written in *Deseret News: Semi-Weekly*, July 20, 1875 (Salt Lake City: The Church of Jesus Christ of Latter-day Saints, 1866–1922), 1; emphasis added; see also *Teachings of Presidents of the Church: Wilford Woodruff* (Salt Lake City: The Church of Jesus Christ of Latter-day Saints, 2004), 84.

5. Ibid., 84

6. Ibid., 84–85.

7. LeGrand Richards, "Laying a Foundation for the Millennium," in Conference Report, October 2, 1971, 85; see also *Ensign*, December 1971, 81.

8. Smith, "Vision of the Celestial Kingdom," *Teachings of the Prophet Joseph Smith,* 107; see also Joseph Smith, *History of the Church of Jesus Christ of Latter-day Saints*, edited by B. H. Roberts, 7 vols. (Salt Lake City: Deseret Book, 1973), 2:381. Note: The Lord has revealed that the age of accountability is eight years of age (see D&C 68:27).

9. Joseph Fielding Smith, *Doctrines of Salvation*, compiled by Bruce R. McConkie, 3 vols. (Salt Lake City: Bookcraft, 1954–56), 2:54; emphasized words already in the quotation.

10. Ibid., 2:54–55; emphasized words already in the quotation.

11. Remarks at the funeral of Daniel Wells Grant, child of Elder and Sister Grant, in family residence, Salt Lake City, Utah, March 12, 1895. See Joseph F. Smith, *Gospel Doctrine: Selections from the Sermons and Writings of Joseph F. Smith* (Salt Lake City: Deseret

Book, 1971), 452; see also *Young Woman's Journal*, March 1895, 6:369–74.

12. Ibid., 452–53.

13. Ibid., 453.

14. Ibid.

15. Ibid., 454.

16. Ibid., 455.

17. Joseph Fielding Smith, "The Administration of President Joseph F. Smith," *Essentials in Church History*, 27th ed. (Salt Lake City: Deseret Book, 1974), 507–18. See also *The Presidents of the Church: Biographical Essays*, edited by Leonard J. Arrington (Salt Lake City: Deseret Book, 1986), 179–209.

18. Joseph F. Smith, "Personal Letterbooks," page 348, film reel #10; historical department of The Church of Jesus Christ of Latter-day Saints, Ms. F 271.

19. Charles W. Penrose, *Deseret News: Semi-Weekly*, February 28, 1918, 2:10; emphasis added.

20. Ibid.

21. Ibid.

22. Orson Pratt, *The Seer*, Washington, DC edition, March 1853, Vol. 1, No. 3, 36.

23. Heber C. Kimball, funeral of Jedediah M. Grant, Dec. 4, 1856. See also *Journal of Discourses*, 26 vols. (London: Latter-day Saints Book Depot, 1854–86), 4:136.

24. Smith, *Gospel Doctrine*, 455; emphasis added.

25. Ibid.

26. Ibid.

27. Ibid.

28. Bryant S. Hinckley, *Sermons and Missionary Services of Melvin Joseph Ballard*, 18th ed. (Salt Lake City: Deseret Book, 1973), 260; emphasis added.

29. Smith, *Gospel Doctrine*, 455–56; emphasis added.

30. Ibid., 456.

31. Ibid.

32. Ibid., 456–57.

33. Ibid., 457.

34. Ibid., 455–56.

35. Smith, *Doctrines of Salvation*, 2:56; emphasized words already in the quotation.

36. Ibid., 57; emphasized words already in the quotation.

CHAPTER 7

# STILLBORN CHILDREN

## MISCARRIAGE OF A FETUS

From the days of Adam to the present, a myriad of women have experienced an early *miscarriage of a fetus*[1] or have had a *fallopian tube pregnancy—generally called a tubal pregnancy—that has also resulted in a miscarriage.*[2] When a *fetus*—described as *a developing human*[3]—is born dead, it is defined as a *stillbirth.*[4] This occurrence has also been defined as a *miscarriage, before the fetus is viable*—that is, before it could have lived on its own outside the mother's womb without artificial support.[5]

Whatever terminology is used, this event has caused many family members who belong to The Church of Jesus Christ of Latter-day Saints to wonder about the status of the fetus. These searching questions are generally asked: (1) Did the fetus become a living soul—wherein the spirit and the body were united in a temporary union?[6] (2) Will a stillborn or miscarried baby be resurrected? And, (3) Will parents eventually be able to raise these little ones?

The revelations given to the Prophet Joseph Smith have not explained why these events take place in the life of women, or what transpires with the fetus in the eternal plan of our Heavenly Father. However, leaders of The Church of Jesus Christ of

Latter-day Saints have either spoken or written encouraging and uplifting counsel on this subject.

Regarding the death of a fetus, President Brigham Young said:

> But suppose an accident occurs and the spirit has to leave this body prematurely, what then? All that the physician says is—"it is a still birth," and that is all they know about it; *but whether the spirit remains in the body a minute, an hour, a day, a year, or lives there until the body has reached a good old age, it is certain that the time will come when they will be separated*, and the body will return to mother earth.[7]

## WHEN DOES A SPIRIT ENTER ITS BODY?

Concerning when a spirit enters its mortal body, President Brigham Young expressed the belief that "when the mother feels life come to her infant, it is the spirit entering the body."[8]

In the masterful document "The Origin of Man," written by the First Presidency in 1909 (Joseph F. Smith, John R. Winder, and Anthon H. Lund), it states:

> The body of man enters upon its career as a tiny germ or embryo, which becomes an infant, quickened at a certain stage by the spirit whose tabernacle it is, and the child, after being born, develops into a man.[9]

There are various opinions on when quickening occurs before a child is born in mortality. Some believe a spirit enters at the time of conception and the spirit makes the fetus develop in its mother's womb. Others believe that the spirit does not enter until the child takes its first breath of life. Admittedly, the revelations have not defined when the spirit enters the body. All that is officially stated—as written by the First Presidency—is a spirit enters the body prior to a normal birth.

President Joseph Fielding Smith, then a member of the Quorum of the Twelve Apostles, expressed his opinion *"that these little ones will receive a resurrection and then belong to us."*

Stillborn children should not be reported nor recorded as births and deaths on the records of the Church, but it is suggested that parents record in their own family records a name for each such stillborn child.[10]

In harmony with this teaching, the Prophet Joseph Smith solemnly declared:

All your losses will be made up to you in the resurrection [of the dead], provided you continue faithful. By the vision of the Almighty I have seen it.[11]

## CONCLUSION

Therefore, worthy parents can trust in the Lord to reward them for their sacrifices and trials experienced in mortality. All that is revealed—and it is a joyous statement that provides hope—is this: "And *not one hair, neither mote [a small particle],*[12] *shall be lost, for it is the workmanship of [the Lord's] hand"* (D&C 29:25; emphasis added).

---

## NOTES

1. *Merriam-Webster's Collegiate Dictionary,* 10th ed. (Springfield, Massachusetts: Merriam-Webster, 2000), 741; emphasis added.
2. Ibid., 916, 1266; emphasis added.
3. Ibid., 430, 741; emphasis added.
4. Ibid., 1152; emphasis added.
5. Ibid., 741, 1310; emphasis added.
6. Abraham 5:7; D&C 88:15.
7. Brigham Young speaking at the funeral services of Thomas Williams, Salt Lake City, Sunday morning, July 19, 1874. See *Journal*

*of Discourses*, 26 vols. (London: Latter-day Saints Book Depot, 1854–86), 17:143; emphasis added.

8. Ibid., 17:143; punctuation modernized.

9. Joseph Fielding Smith, *Man: His Origin and Destiny* (Salt Lake City: Deseret Book, 1954), 354. See also *Messages of the First Presidency of The Church of Jesus Christ of Latter-day Saints*, compiled by James R. Clark (Salt Lake City: Bookcraft, 1970), 4:205.

10. Joseph Fielding Smith, *Doctrines of Salvation*, 3 vols., compiled by Bruce R. McConkie (Salt Lake City: Bookcraft, 1954–56), 2:280; emphasized words already in the quotation.

11. Joseph Smith, *Teachings of the Prophet Joseph Smith*, selected by Joseph Fielding Smith (Salt Lake City: Deseret Book, 1976), 296.

12. *Merriam-Webster's Collegiate Dictionary*, 757; emphasis added.

## CHAPTER 8

# PARADISE AND SPIRIT PRISON

## DEFINING PARADISE

An informative conversation is recorded in the Book of Mormon between Alma and one of his sons concerning the resurrection of the dead. The prophet told Corianton that there is a space appointed between death and the Resurrection when all shall rise from the dead (see Alma 40:1–6). Alma then tells what became of the souls of men between death and the Resurrection. An angel had made known to him that when the spirits of mankind, as soon as they are departed from their mortal bodies, they are taken *home* to their God who gave them life. The spirits of the righteous are received into a state of happiness called *paradise*, which is a place of peace where they rest from all their troubles, care, and sorrow (see Alma 40:7–12).

From Alma's explanation, an individual learns that *paradise* is the temporary *home* of righteous spirits pending the day of their resurrection. Therefore, paradise is not the ultimate *home* of righteous spirits; it is, however, a *home* of peace and rest; it is the temporary *home* designated as the space appointed between death and the Resurrection (Alma 40:5–6, 9).

Speaking of the spirit world, President Joseph Fielding Smith, then a member of the Quorum of the Twelve Apostles, said:

When men [and women] die they do not go into the presence of God, they do not go into the celestial kingdom. Where do they go? *They go into the world of spirits, the righteous into paradise*, where they await the resurrection. It is not until after the resurrection that they shall enter into their exaltation.[1]

Later in his address, President Smith emphasized this teaching:

Now let us keep it clearly in our minds that we do not enter into exaltation until after the resurrection. We do not enter into exaltation in the spirit world.[2]

In the New Testament it is written that the Lord told one of the thieves on the cross: "To day shalt thou be with me in *paradise*" (Luke 23:43; emphasis added). In the Joseph Smith Translation it is written: "And the Lord said unto him, This day thou shalt be with me in *Paradise*" (Matthew 27:48; emphasis added). Revealing insightful knowledge, the Prophet Joseph Smith gave this explanation concerning these passages of scripture:

King James' translators make it out to say *paradise*. But what is paradise? It is a modern word: it does not answer at all to the original word that Jesus made use of . . . There is nothing in the original word in Greek from which this was taken that signifies paradise; but it was—*This day thou shalt be with me in the world of spirits.*[3]

Later in his discourse, the Prophet stated:

I will now turn linguist. *There are many things in the Bible which do not, as they now stand, accord with the revelations of the Holy Ghost to me . . .*

Hades, the Greek, or Sheol, the Hebrew, these two significations mean a world of spirits. Hades, Sheol, *paradise*, spirits in prison, are all one: *it is a world of spirits.*[4]

In the New Testament it is written that Paul—who was called to be a member of the Jewish Twelve Apostles[5]—had a spiritual experience where he was "caught up to the *third heaven*." Paul also says "he was caught up into *paradise*, and heard unspeakable words, which it is not lawful for a man to utter" (2 Corinthians 12:2, 4; emphasis added).

To better understand these passages of scripture, we turn again to the Prophet Joseph Smith for information:

> Paul ascended into the third heavens, and he could understand the three principle rounds of Jacob's ladder—the telestial, the terrestrial, and the celestial glories or kingdoms, where Paul saw and heard things which were not lawful for him to utter. I could explain a hundred fold more than I ever have of the glories of the kingdoms manifested to me in the vision, were I permitted, and were the people prepared to receive them.[6]

Concerning Paul's spiritual experience, the Prophet Joseph Smith spoke these short but meaningful words: *"Paul saw the third heavens, and I more."*[7]

Thus, Paul was caught up to the celestial kingdom. From what Alma said, as written in the Book of Mormon, paradise is not the third heaven. It is that part of the spirit world where the righteous spirits go to await the day of their resurrection. With this stated, it should be noted that the scriptural account of Paul's spiritual experience says that he was "caught up to the third heaven" and "into paradise" (2 Corinthians 12:2, 4). In one of his many published books, Elder Bruce R. McConkie, then a member of the First Council of the Seventy, wrote this sentence:

> If our account of Paul's experience is accurately preserved to us, it means that he was *caught up to the celestial kingdom* and *to the paradise of God*, a thing which is entirely probable.[8]

From the words spoken by the Prophet Joseph Smith, the word *paradise* as written in the King James Version of the Bible means the *world of spirits.*[9] Therefore, the thief on the cross was told he would go that day to the *world of spirits.* In addition, Paul was caught up to the celestial kingdom and probably the *world of spirits.* As written in the Book of Mormon, Alma states that the spirits of the righteous are received into a state of happiness called *paradise*, which is a place of peace where they rest from all their troubles, cares, and sorrows (see Alma 40:11–12). Thus, the *dual meaning* of the word *paradise* is correctly defined by Alma and the Prophet Joseph Smith.

## DEFINING SPIRIT PRISON

The word *spirit prison* has two distinct meanings. Each meaning will be discussed in the following subheadings.

## DEFINITION ONE—ABODE OF RIGHTEOUS SPIRITS

Until righteous disembodied spirits receive their bodies in the Resurrection, they consider their habitation in this realm as one of imprisonment.

While speaking in the Tabernacle, President Brigham Young asked and answered the following questions:

> Where are the *spirits of the ungodly? They are in prison.* Where are the *spirits of the righteous,* the Prophets, and the Apostles? *They are in prison*, brethren; that is where they are.[10]

Knowing that some in the congregation would be surprised at his comments, President Young provided this explanation:

> I know it is a startling idea to say that the Prophet [meaning Joseph Smith] *and the persecutor of the Prophet, all go to prison together . . . but they have not got their bodies yet, consequently they are in prison.*[11]

In addition to the words spoken by President Young, Elder Orson Pratt also asked and answered these questions:

> When our spirits leave these bodies, will they be happy? Not perfectly so. Why? *Because the spirit is absent from the body;* it cannot be perfectly happy while a part of the man [or woman] is lying in the earth . . . *You will be happy, you will be at ease in paradise; but still you will be looking for a house [body] where your spirit can enter, and act as you did in former times.*[12]

In harmony with the teachings of President Young and Elder Pratt, Elder Bruce R. McConkie, then a member of the First Council of the Seventy, wrote these words:

> Since disembodied spirits cannot gain a fulness of joy until their resurrection (D&C 93:33–34), they consider their habitation in the spirit world as one of imprisonment, and so the whole spirit world (including both paradise and hell) is a *spirit prison*. It was to the *righteous spirits in prison*, those who were in paradise, that our Lord preached while his body was in the tomb" (1 Peter 3:18–21; 4:6; D&C 76:73–74).[13]

As revealed in the revelations, the disembodied spirits long for deliverance and seek for relief from their present condition in the spirit world; they look upon the long absence of their spirits from their physical body as a bondage (see D&C 45:17; 138:50).

Paraphrasing what Elder Orson Pratt taught, *spirits in paradise will be happy and at ease*, but they *will be looking for their body where their spirit can enter* and act as in former times.[14] From these teachings, the first meaning of spirit prison is correctly defined.

## DEFINITION TWO—ABODE OF WICKED SPIRITS

That part of the spirit world inhabited by wicked disembodied spirits is called hell.

In the Book of Mormon, Alma was also told by an angel "*the spirits of the wicked*, yea, who are evil . . . [are in] a state of awful, fearful looking for the fiery indignation of the wrath of God upon them; *thus they remain in this state, as well as the righteous in paradise, until the time of their resurrection*" (Alma 40:13–14; emphasis added).

In the Pearl of Great Price, the Lord told Enoch that "*a prison have I prepared*" for the "*wicked*" (Moses 7:38, 43; emphasis added).

In a grand vision given to the Prophet Joseph Smith and

Sidney Rigdon, 1832, the following statement is written regarding the wicked: "These are they who are cast down to *hell*" (D&C 76:106; emphasis added). Combining these scriptural statements, the following conclusion can be made: *That part of the spirit world inhabited by the wicked awaiting the day of their resurrection is called hell.* From these scriptural references, the second meaning of spirit prison is correctly defined.

---

NOTES

1. Joseph Fielding Smith, address given December 30, 1934. See *Utah Genealogical and Historical Magazine* (Salt Lake City: Genealogical Society of Utah, April 1935), 26:59; emphasis added.
2. Ibid., 61.
3. Joseph Smith, *Teachings of the Prophet Joseph Smith*, selected by Joseph Fielding Smith (Salt Lake City: Deseret Book, 1976), 309; emphasis added. See also Joseph Smith, *History of The Church of Jesus Christ of Latter-day Saints*, 7 vols., edited by B. H. Roberts (Salt Lake City: Deseret Book, 1974), 5:424–25.
4. Smith, *Teachings of the Prophet Joseph Smith*, 310; emphasis added; see also Smith, *History of the Church*, 5:425.
5. 1 Corinthians 1:1; 2 Corinthians 1:1; Galatians 1:1–24; Ephesians 1:1; 1 Timothy 1:1; 2:7; 2 Timothy 1:1; Titus 1:1; see also statements written by Joseph Fielding Smith, *Doctrines of Salvation*, compiled by Bruce R. McConkie, 3 vols. (Salt Lake City: Bookcraft, 1954–56), 3:153, and Bruce R. McConkie, *Doctrinal New Testament Commentary*, 3 vols. (Salt Lake City: Bookcraft, 1965–73), 2:131.
6. Smith, *Teachings of the Prophet Joseph Smith*, 304–5; emphasis added. See also Smith, *History of the Church*, 5:402.
7. Smith, *Teachings of the Prophet Joseph Smith*, 301; emphasis added. See also Smith, *History of the Church*, 5:392.

8. McConkie, *Doctrinal New Testament Commentary*, 2:447; emphasis added.

9. Smith, *Teachings of the Prophet Joseph Smith*, 309; emphasis added. See also Smith, *History of The Church*, 5:424–25.

10. Brigham Young, *Journal of Discourses*, 26 vols. (London: Latter-day Saints Book Depot, 1854–86), 3:95; emphasis added.

11. Ibid.; emphasis added.

12. Orson Pratt, *Journal of Discourses*, 1:289; emphasis added.

13. Bruce R. McConkie, *Mormon Doctrine*, 2nd ed. (Salt Lake City: Bookcraft, 1966), 755.

14. Orson Pratt, *Journal of Discourses*, 1:289; emphasis added.

CHAPTER 9

# THE WORLD OF
# SEPARATED SPIRITS

## LOCATION OF THE SPIRIT WORLD

When physical death occurs, a spirit leaves its mortal body and goes directly into the spirit world. Concerning this event, the Prophet Joseph Smith spoke these uplifting words:

> The spirits of the just are exalted to a greater and more glorious work; *hence they are blessed in their departure to the world of spirits.* Enveloped in flaming fire, *they are not far from us,* and know and understand our thoughts, feelings, and motions, and are often pained therewith.[1]

President Brigham Young asked this searching question: "Is the *spirit world* here?" Answering, he revealed this knowledge, "It is not beyond the sun, *but is on this earth* that was organized for the people that have lived and that do and will live upon it."[2]

Elder Parley P. Pratt, a member of the Quorum of the Twelve Apostles, wrote this description of the spirit world: "As to its location, it is here on the very planet where we were born."[3]

In complete agreement with these statements, President Harold B. Lee, then a member of the Quorum of the Twelve Apostles, said: "The spirit world isn't on another planet millions of miles away. *The spirit world is right here on this earth.*"[4]

Therefore, it is plainly taught that the spirit world is not far away, it is here on this earth. Elder Alvin R. Dyer, then an Assistant to the Quorum of the Twelve Apostles, wrote these informative words concerning the spirit world:

> *There is a veil between the one sphere and the other* which renders the spiritual sphere invisible to the temporal. *To discern beings or things in the spirit world, a person in the flesh [mortality] must be quickened by spiritual element*; the veil must be drawn, or the organs of sight, or of hearing, must be transformed, so as to be adapted to the spiritual sphere.[5]

## Many Subdivisions in the Spirit World

In a Church publication, Elder Charles W. Penrose, then a member of the Quorum of the Twelve Apostles, wrote a significant description of the spirit world:

> There are conditions of spirit life between death and the resurrection. There are *two grand divisions* in the spirit world; the good gravitate to and associate with the good; the bad with the bad. *There are doubtless many subdivisions in each of these spirit spheres*, according to the various grades and qualities of the individuals and their course of life when in the body. *They are capable of receiving information, can exercise faith, repentance and obedience, or take an opposite course.* Volition, or will power, is an attribute of the spirit of man, and that is why he is responsible for his conduct whether in the body or out of the body, and why, therefore, he will be brought to judgment, and his eternal status will be "according to his works."
>
> The portion of the spirit world where the good dwell between death and the resurrection, is sometimes called *paradise*, and that where the evil abide is called hades, or *hell*. Memory, which is a quality of the spirit, will be complete in that state, and will bring joy to the righteous and inexpressible sorrow to the wicked. The former, who have obeyed the truth and walked in its light, obtained forgiveness of sin and received the witness of the Holy Ghost, await with joy the time when they shall receive their bodies again, quickened after the power of an endless life

to inherit glory in the presence of God and Christ in worlds without end. The latter linger in doubt and uncertainty concerning their future and the results of the judgment.[6]

## PARTIAL JUDGMENT

In harmony with the words of Elder Penrose, President Joseph F. Smith taught this truth:

> The spirits of all men [and women], as soon as they depart from this mortal body, whether they are good or evil, we are told in the Book of Mormon, are taken home to that God who gave them life, where there is a separation, a *partial judgment*, and the spirits of those who are righteous are received into a state of happiness which is called paradise . . . . The wicked, on the contrary . . . are cast into outer darkness [described in the scriptures as "hell"[7]].[8]

By this "partial judgment," every spirit will be assigned a place in the spirit world for which the earth-life of the individual has qualified it. The final judgment will not take place until the Resurrection, when an individual will be brought to stand before God and be judged according to his or her works.[9]

## THE ABRAHAMIC COVENANT

As will be presented, the descendants of Abraham who die without receiving the gospel in mortality have claim upon their birthright in the life to come. Regardless of their literal blood line, individuals who become members of the Church are adopted into the lineage of Abraham.

The restoration of the gospel of Jesus Christ in these latter days directly relates with the great promises made to Abraham of the Old Testament. One promise was that through him and his seed after him all the nations of the earth would be blessed (see Genesis 12:1–3; Abraham 2:9–11).

This promise was made known to the Prophet Joseph Smith

by revelation as early as 1831 but was not recorded until 1843, that:

> Abraham received promises concerning his seed . . . from whose loins ye are, namely, my servant Joseph . . . and as touching Abraham and his seed, out of the world they should continue; *both in the world and out of the world should they continue* as innumerable as the stars; or, if ye were to count the sand upon the seashore ye could not number them. (D&C 132:30; emphasis added)

In addition to this revelation, the Prophet Joseph Smith said:

> For as the Holy Ghost falls upon one of the literal seed of Abraham [in mortality], it is calm and serene . . . *while the effect of the Holy Ghost upon a Gentile, is to purge out the old blood, and make him actually of the seed of Abraham.* That man [or woman] that has none of the blood of Abraham (naturally) must have a new creation by the Holy Ghost.[10]

Thus, individuals who receive the Holy Ghost by complying with the ordinances of the gospel of Jesus Christ, no matter what their literal blood line might be, are adopted into the lineage of Abraham. This law of adoption applies to both those who live upon the earth and those who reside in the spirit world (see Matthew 3:9–10; Matthew 8:10–12; Jacob 5).

The covenant that God made with Abraham was that the posterity of all mankind would be entitled to the blessings of the gospel of Jesus Christ. These blessings include the *priesthood, celestial marriage, and eternal life* (see D&C 132:30; D&C 10:50; D&C 84:33–44; D&C 133:62).

As revealed in these writings, the blessings given to the posterity of Abraham has such a binding effect that mortal death cannot remove it. The descendants of Abraham who die without receiving the gospel have claim upon their birthright in the life to come. In the world of spirits they will be taught the gospel of Jesus Christ by those righteous spirits (as taught by Alma) who are also of Abraham's seed. Once these individuals embrace the gospel, through the ordinances performed in the temple on earth by those who act as proxy for them, each will receive all of the promised blessings of Abraham.

## A PREPARED PLACE IN THE SPIRIT WORLD

Reiterating the teaching by President Joseph F. Smith concerning a partial judgment of spirits, Elder Joseph F. Merrill, a member of the Quorum of the Twelve Apostles, expressed this teaching concerning the spirit world:

> When death comes the departed spirit, a personal entity of the form of the earthly body, is conducted to a prepared place in the *spirit world*. Here the spirit, a knowing, intelligent personal being, will live until the day of the Resurrection.
>
> *It is important to understand that the spirits of the dead do not all go to the same place. The spirits of saints and sinners, for example, cannot live together.* Each spirit goes to a place for which the earth-life of the individual has qualified it to dwell. *The wicked will not live in realms of joy, but saints will—the degree of joy or sorrow of everyone who dies being governed by his merits.*[11]

In agreement with this statement, Elder Orson F. Whitney wrote this description:

> There are two classes of beings in the Spirit World . . . Good and bad spirits inhabit that realm. *Light and darkness divide it*, and each domain has its appropriate population.[12]

Providing additional information, Elder Orson Pratt penned these words:

> Those in [spirit] prison are in an intermediate state: they are not saved, neither are they irrecoverably lost: *but when the gospel is preached to them it will decide their fate*, redeeming those who receive it, and damning those who reject it; the one rising to light, glory, and happiness—and the other falling to darkness, damnation, and misery.

Q. Is this intermediate state, which is called in the scriptures a prison, a place of punishment?

A. Yes: but the severity of the punishment is not as great as is experienced among those who are sent to hell. *Their punishment will be in proportion to their sins and the light which they have rejected.* Indeed, the long ages of darkness, ignorance, doubt, and uncertainty which will slowly roll away, will of itself make them wretched and miserable. How tedious and wearisome must have been the condition of the antediluvian[13] spirits [before the flood in Noah's day] to remain the long period of two thousand years and upwards without any ray of hope, *until Jesus opened their prison doors, by preaching the gospel to them while his body was sleeping in the tomb.*[14]

Concerning the words written by Elder Pratt, it is written in the New Testament that Peter, who was the senior member of the Jewish Twelve Apostles,[15] wrote that Christ *"went and preached unto the spirits in prison"* who *"were disobedient"* (1 Peter 3:18–20; emphasis added). "For this *cause was the gospel preached also to them that are dead*, that they might be judged according to men in the flesh, but live according to God *in the spirit"* (1 Peter 4:6; emphasis added).

## VISION OF THE REDEMPTION OF THE DEAD

These statements are clarified in the vision of the redemption of the dead that was seen by President Joseph F. Smith in October 1918. President Smith saw that during our Savior's visit to the spirits in prison, *"the Lord went not in person among the wicked and the disobedient* who had rejected the truth" (D&C 138:29), but that He went "declaring liberty to the captives who had been faithful" (D&C 138:18), a vast multitude of righteous spirits, who were "gathered together in one place" (D&C 138:12). While there, our Lord "preached to them the everlasting gospel" (D&C 138:19). When this was accomplished, "*from among the righteous [spirits],*" our Savior, "organized his forces and appointed messengers, clothed with power and authority, *and commissioned them to go forth and carry the light of the gospel to them that were in darkness, even to all the spirits of men [and women]*" (D&C 138:30).

Providing additional information, Elder Bruce R. McConkie, then a member of the First Council of the Seventy, adequately explained this teaching:

> Before Christ bridged the gulf between paradise and hell—so that the righteous could mingle with the wicked and preach them the gospel—the wicked in hell were confined to locations which precluded them from contact with the righteous in paradise.[16]

## A Diversity of Spirits

There are variations of righteous spirits in paradise, so also there are differences among those spirits who are in hell. In support of this statement, President George Q. Cannon of the First Presidency provided this explanation:

> There will be as *many differences between the spirits in the spirit world* as there are differences today in *spirits that are upon the earth*—some who are worthy of celestial glory, some who are worthy of the terrestrial glory, and some who are only worthy of the telestial glory, of which the stars are a similitude. *There is this difference in the human family, and this arises from the fact that we all have our agency.* We all have the power given unto us to obey, or disobey, to rise or not to rise. You see this in families; you see it in brothers, born of the same parents; you see it in sisters. *All these differences will always exist to a greater or less extent throughout eternity.*[17]

Providing information, Elder Alvin R. Dyer, then an Assistant to the Quorum of the Twelve Apostles, wrote this description:

> "The spirit world will contain the same cross-section of diversity of race and creed that exist upon the earth. The spirit

will awaken there with the same religious concept, or the lack of it. There will be Catholics and Protestants of every sect, Jews, Mohammedans, Hindus, Buddhists, and others as well as the infidels [those who acknowledge no religious belief[18]].[19]

## Gospel Taught by Righteous Spirits

As revealed in the vision of the redemption of the dead given to President Joseph F. Smith in 1918, the righteous spirits were commissioned by the Lord to carry the message of the gospel to the wicked spirits in spirit prison (see D&C 138:30–37). Six years previous to President Smith receiving this significant vision, he expressed this belief:

> I have always believed, and still do believe with all my soul that such men as *Peter and James, and the twelve disciples chosen of the Savior in His time,* have been engaged all the centuries that have passed since their martyrdom for the testimony of Jesus Christ, *in proclaiming liberty to the captives in the spirit world and in opening their prison doors.*[20]

## World Population

Speaking in a general conference in 1949, Elder Richard L. Evans, then a member of the First Council of Seventy, spoke these informative words:

> One of the things that happens in this world every day of which I think we are not too well aware is the *going and coming of tens of thousands of people*—the arrivals of newcomers and the departures of those who have finished their sojourn here [on earth], for a time at least. It is an ever startling fact to me that about one hundred fifty thousand people arrive in this world every day, and that *more than eighty thousand leave this world every day.*[21]

According to Wikipedia,

> The world population is the total number of living humans

on Earth at a given time. As of 12 May 2010, the Earth's population is estimated by the United States Census Bureau to be 6,820,400,000. . . . World births have leveled off at about 134 million per year. . . . However, deaths are only around fifty-seven million per year, and are expected to increase to ninety million by the year 2050.[22]

Therefore, from 1949 to 2010, the *world death rate* has increased from more than 80,000 to around *156,000 people a day*. As Elder Evans expressed it, this is an "ever startling fact." In 1992, Elder Russell M. Nelson, a member of the Quorum of the Twelve Apostles and a renowned heart surgeon, said that "sixty-nine billion people" have lived on this earth.[23] From 1992 to 2010, that number has increased measurably. From these calculated numbers, can one imagine the number of spirits who reside in paradise and in hell? The numbers are truly "startling." Think what that means in terms of reaching and teaching the true gospel of Jesus Christ to billions of spirits who are in spirit prison, and those numbers increase by approximately 156,000 spirits a day.

## ORDER AND ORGANIZATION IN THE SPIRIT WORLD

With the vast number of spirits residing and arriving daily in the world of spirits, one must believe that the spirit world is a very orderly and organized place of habitation. Though the revelations in the Doctrine and Covenants do not specifically mention the world of spirits, they support the belief that all things are governed by order. It is written in one, "all things may be done in order" (20:68); in another, "an everlasting order" (82:20); and specifically in one, "for my house is a house of order" (132:18). In total agreement with the words quoted in these revelations, President Heber C. Kimball, then First Counselor in the First Presidency, speaking at the funeral of President Jedediah M. Grant, who was the Second Counselor in the First Presidency, said:

He [a dying President Grant] said to me, brother Heber,

I have been *into the spirit world two nights in succession.* . . . But O, says he, *the order and government that were there*! When in the spirit world, I saw the order of righteous men and women; beheld them *organized in their several grades*, and there appeared to be no obstruction to my vision; I could see every man and woman in their grade and order. *I looked to see whether there was any disorder there, but there was none*; neither could I see any death nor any darkness, disorder or confusion. *He said that the people he there saw were organized in family capacities*; and when he looked at them he saw grade after grade, *and all were organized and in perfect harmony.*[24]

## FAMILY HISTORY SEARCH

In harmony with the statement made by President Kimball that President Grant said he saw that "people were organized in family capacities," President George Q. Cannon, then First Counselor in the First Presidency, emphasized this important teaching in 1880:

*We cannot have our dead [in each family] redeemed*, we cannot ourselves be prepared for the exaltation that awaits us *unless we attend to these matters in accordance with the law of God respecting them.* There are generations [of families] to be looked after. For 1,400 years, the people on this [American] Continent were without the [true] Gospel, and the power of the Priesthood, and, indeed, so far as that is concerned, it is nearly 1,800 years since the Priesthood was upon the earth; *and the salvation of the unnumbered millions [more correctly billions] of people who have lived since that period will have to be cared for.* Trace, if you can, your own [family] genealogy back only a few generations, and see how it spreads out on every point. For instance, for one mother we have two grandmothers, four great grandmothers, and eight great, great grandmothers, etc. And thus it spreads out like the branches of a tree, until all of the inhabitants of the earth will be brought in . . . In the Temples that shall be built, you [as a temple recommend holder] will have the opportunity of standing therein, as saviors, upon Mount Zion. That is your calling; and it is your privilege to be saviors on Mount Zion . . . *It is your duty now to rise up, all of you, and trace your genealogies,* and begin to exercise the powers which belong to saviors of men, and when you do this in earnest, you will begin to comprehend how widespread, how numerous your [family] ancestors are, *for whom Temple work has to be performed, in order that they may be brought into the fold*; and when you get stopped, the Lord will reveal further information to you; *and in this way the work of salvation and redemption will be accomplished, even from Father Adam down to the last one.*[25]

## DISPENSATION OF THE FULNESS OF TIMES

When the disembodied Savior visited the spirit world, the important and necessary work of the redemption of the dead began at that time. From the Apostle Paul's first epistle to the Corinthians it is made known that the former-day Saints had began vicarious baptisms for the dead (1 Corinthians 15:29), and it is believed that such work continued until the great apostasy took place, approximately seventy or eighty years after the mortal death of our Savior and the Jewish Twelve Apostles. From that time—which was the dispensation of Christ—until the restored gospel of Jesus Christ was revealed to the Prophet Joseph Smith, the responsibility for vicarious ordinances rests with this final dispensation, called the dispensation of the fulness of times (D&C 27:13). In a well-researched book about the Prophet Joseph Smith, Brothers Joseph Fielding McConkie and Robert L. Millet wrote these brief but profound words:

> Think of it! Joseph Smith and his successors are responsible for teaching the gospel in the world of spirits and for performing saving ordinances for literally billions of our Father's children.[26]

As was written in chapter three, President Wilford Woodruff said,

*Joseph Smith visited me a great deal after his death*, and taught me many important principles . . . *The last time I saw him was in heaven. In the night vision I saw him at the door of the temple in heaven. He came to me and spoke to me.* He said he could not stop to talk with me because he was in a hurry. . . *I met half a dozen brethren who had held high positions on earth*, and none of them could stop to talk with me because they were in a hurry . . . By and by I saw the Prophet again and I got the privilege of asking him a question.

"Now," said I, "I want to know why you are in a hurry."

Joseph Said: "I will tell you, Brother Woodruff . . . We are the last dispensation, and so much work has to be done, and we need to be in a hurry in order to accomplish it."[27]

With "so much work" to be done in preaching the true gospel of Jesus Christ to billions of spirits in spirit prison and around 156,000 spirits arriving daily, it cannot be accomplished solely by the Prophet Joseph Smith and those faithful elders in his day. As President Joseph F. Smith saw in the vision of the redemption of the dead, he:

*Beheld that the faithful elders of this dispensation, when they depart from mortal life, continue their labors in the preaching of the gospel of repentance and redemption*, through the sacrifice of the Only Begotten Son of God, among those who are in darkness and under the *bondage of sin in the great world of the spirits of the dead. The dead who repent will be redeemed, through obedience to the ordinances of the house of God.* (D&C 138:57–58; emphasis added; see also D&C 124:39)

In harmony with this vision, Elder Bruce R. McConkie has written these significant words:

Why preach the gospel in the spirit world unless believing souls in that realm can repent and be saved? . . . The judgments of God are just because of salvation for the dead. If the dead could not be saved on the same basis as the living, God would be neither just nor merciful, and thus would cease to be God.[28]

Reiterating what was previously written in this chapter: In the scriptures, the blessings given to the posterity of Abraham have such a binding effect that mortal death cannot remove them. Therefore, the descendants of Abraham who die without receiving the gospel have claim upon their birthright in the life to come. In the world of spirits they will be taught the gospel of Jesus Christ by those righteous spirits (as taught by Alma) who are also of Abraham's seed. Once these individuals embrace the gospel, through the ordinances performed in the temple on earth by those who act as proxy for them, each will receive all of the promised blessings of Abraham.

## CONCLUSION

The spirit world is a temporary home for all of mankind. For those in paradise, it is a place where they shall rest from all their troubles, care, and sorrow. Faithful elders will be busy preaching the gospel of repentance to those spirits who are in darkness and under the bondage of sin. With agency in full force, those spirits in hell who accept the true gospel of Jesus Christ and have the saving ordinances of the gospel performed in the temple on earth by those who act as proxy for them are permitted to cross the gulf that separates the two spirit realms and enjoy the sweet and peaceful association with the faithful spirits in paradise, awaiting the promised resurrection from the dead.

---

NOTES

1. Joseph Smith, *Teachings of the Prophet Joseph Smith*, selected by Joseph Fielding Smith (Salt Lake City: Deseret Book, 1976), 326; emphasis added.

2. Brigham Young, *Journal of Discourses*, 26 vols. (London: Latter-day Saints Book Depot, 1854–86), 3:372; emphasis added.

3. Parley P. Pratt, *Key to the Science of Theology*, 3rd ed. (Salt Lake City: Deseret News, 1883), 129–30.

4. Harold B. Lee, "Funeral Services for Mable Hale Forsey," October 24, 1960; typewritten copy, page 12; emphasis added.

5. Alvin R. Dyer, *Who Am I?* (Salt Lake City: Deseret Book, 1963) 501–2; emphasis added.

6. Charles W. Penrose, *The Millennial Star*, March 14, 1907, 69:168–69; emphasis added. See also *Journal of Discourses*, 23:161. He also taught: "The spirits of the wicked will gravitate together, while the righteous will go to their place in the paradise of God."

7. 1 Nephi 15:29; 2 Nephi 9:12, 34; 28:15; D&C 76:84–85.

8. Joseph F. Smith, *Improvement Era*, June 1914, 7:619; as written in Joseph F. Smith, *Gospel Doctrine: Selections from the Sermons and Writings of Joseph F. Smith* (Salt Lake City: Deseret Book, 1971), 448; emphasis added.

9. Ibid.

10. Smith, *Teachings of the Prophet Joseph Smith*, 149–50; emphasis added.

11. Joseph F. Merrill, *The Millennial Star*, February 13, 1936, 98:104; emphasis added.

12. Orson F. Whitney, *The Millennial Star*, January 26, 1922, 84:57; emphasis added.

13. *Merriam-Webster's Collegiate Dictionary*, 10th ed. (Springfield, Massachusetts: Merriam-Webster, 2000), 48.

14. Orson Pratt, "Questions and Answers on Doctrine," *The Seer*, Washington, DC edition, January 1854, Vol. II, No. 1, 208; emphasis added.

15. Matthew 10:1–4; Luke 6:12–16.

16. Bruce R. McConkie, *Mormon Doctrine*, 2nd ed. (Salt Lake City: Bookcraft, 1966), 755.

17. George Q. Cannon, *The Millennial Star*, May 10, 1891, 53:580; emphasis added.

18. *Merriam-Webster's Collegiate Dictionary*, 597.

19. Dyer, *Who Am I?* 490–91.

20. Joseph F. Smith, *Young Woman's Journal*, March 1912, 23:130; emphasis added.

21. Richard L. Evans, in Conference Report, April 3, 1949, 22–23.

22. Wikipedia (www.wikipedia.org), "World Population," accessed November 16, 2010. See also U.S. Census Bureau (www.census.gov).

23. Russell M. Nelson, "Doors of Death," *Ensign*, May 1992, 73.

24. Heber C. Kimball, funeral services of Jedediah M. Grant, Dec. 4, 1856. See *Journal of Discourses*, 4:135–36; emphasis added.

25. George Q. Cannon, *Journal of Discourses*, October 31, 1880, 22:129–30; emphasis added.

26. Joseph Fielding McConkie and Robert L. Millet, *Joseph Smith, the Choice Seer* (Salt Lake City: Bookcraft, 1996), xxvi.

27. Wilford Woodruff, *The Discourses of Wilford Woodruff*, selected by G. Homer Durham (Salt Lake City: Bookcraft, 1969), 288–89.

28. Bruce R. McConkie, *A New Witness for the Articles of Faith* (Salt Lake City: Deseret Book, 1985), 156–57.

## CHAPTER 10

# GRADES OR CLASSES
# OF ANGELS

## TWO KINDS OF BEINGS IN HEAVEN

In February 1843, the Lord revealed the following to the Prophet Joseph Smith:

> There are two kinds of beings in heaven, namely: *Angels, who are resurrected personages*, having bodies of flesh and bones—
>
> For instance, Jesus said: *Handle me and see, for a spirit hath not flesh and bones, as ye see me have.*
>
> Secondly: *the spirits of just men made perfect, they who are not resurrected*, but inherit the same glory. (D&C 129:1–3; emphasis added)

These are the righteous spirits in paradise who were faithful in mortality; these spirit personages are waiting for the day of resurrection, when their spirit and body can be reunited.

In an early Church magazine, edited by President Joseph F. Smith, this *significant explanation* is written concerning these scriptures:

> *It is not asserted that there are no other kinds of persons in heaven than they, but the subject treated is of the two classes mentioned.*
>
> Comparison with other texts of scripture, ancient and modern, *makes clear the fact that there are other grades or classes of*

*heavenly beings than the two spoken of in Section 129.* It is understood by ordinary students of modern religion that there are *perfected beings called gods,* who are higher than the angels (see section 132:16–20), and to whom the angels are servants. And even among the gods there are *Presiding Personages, the Holy Trinity, standing at the head.*

There are angels of various appointments and stations. *Michael is called an "archangel"* (D&C 29:26; Daniel 10:13). Some are resurrected beings like the angel that was sent to John the Revelator (Revelation 23:8, 9) and those already referred to in D&C 132, while others are *"ministering spirits* sent forth to minister unto them who shall be heirs of salvation" (Hebrews 1:14). *Some of these angels are described as "the spirits of just men made perfect"* and are "not resurrected," and *others were made ministering spirits before entering into mortality,* serving among their fellows in their pre-existent state.[1]

Giving specific illustrations, the article continues:

*Christ was a ministering spirit* before his birth into this world. He was "anointed above his fellows." The angel *Gabriel was a ministering spirit* after he had been a mortal man (Noah), and before his resurrection, for Jesus of Nazareth was . . . "the first-fruits of them that slept." (See Luke 1:11–30; Daniel 8:16; 9:21.)[2]

## Premortal or Disembodied Angels

Then, these informative words are written:

*Angels are God's messengers,* whether used in that capacity as *unembodied spirits* [premortal spirits], selected according to their capacities for the work required, or as *disembodied spirits* [righteous spirits in paradise], or as translated men, or as resurrected beings. They are agents of Deity of different degrees or intelligence, power and authority, under the direction of higher dignitaries, and subject to law and order in their respective spheres . . .

*Angels high in authority have been clothed on special occasions with the right to represent Deity personally.* They have appeared and have been recognized as God himself, just as royal ambassadors of earthy potentates have acted, as recorded in [secular] history. The Angel spoken of in Exodus 23:20–22 was one of these. So also was the Angel already spoken of who ministered to John on the isle of Patmos, and used the names and titles of the Son of God. (Revelation 1:1)[3]

## ANGELS DO NOT HAVE WINGS

This article discusses "winged beings."

The popular notion that angels are winged beings, because it is stated by some scripture writers that they saw them "flying through the heavens," is a fallacy. Cherubim and Seraphim spoken of by Ezekiel and Isaiah, are not to be classed with the angels, *for the angels are of the same race and descent as men, whether in body or in spirit, and do not need wings for locomotion [to move or go places], nor do they appear in birdlike form.* They are of the family of Deity in different degrees of progression and are "in the image and likeness" of the Most High.[4]

## FALLEN ANGELS

Concerning "fallen angels," the following is written:

*There are fallen angels, too,* who were cast down for transgression, as mentioned by Jude (verse 6), *chief among whom on this earth is Lucifer or Satan,* who has sought on many occasions to appear as an *"angel of light"* to deceive and lead astray, and who tempted the Son of God, but failed in his efforts as he did with Moses and with the Prophet Joseph Smith (see Luke 4:1–13; Visions of Moses 1:12–22; D&C 128:20). *That great spiritual personage was an angel of God in his "first estate,"* and yet never had a body of flesh, but "was in authority in the presence of God" *as a spirit,* before he rebelled and was "'thrust down." (D&C 76:25–28)[5]

## CONCLUDING STATEMENTS IN ARTICLE

Thus it will be seen that all angels [in heaven] are not resurrected . . . nor is it so declared [in the previously mentioned scriptures from section 129].[6]

Regarding the reference to D&C 130:5, the article says:

In the first place, it is not there declared that no angels from or belonging to other worlds have ever ministered on this earth. The words are in the present tense; that is: "*There are no angels who minister to this earth but those who do belong or have belonged to it.*" That is absolutely correct as it relates to the present and many of the past dispensations. *It may also be true as to the ministrations of heavenly beings to man [or woman] on this earth, ever since the fall [of Adam and Eve].* The angel who spoke to Adam when he offered sacrifice, like the Savior himself, doubtless [also] "belongs to this earth" through receiving a tabernacle [mortal body] here subsequent to his appearance as a "ministering spirit" in the beginning. Abraham, Jeremiah, many others not mentioned in scripture by name, were among "the noble and great ones" chosen before they were born into this world and ministering as required under the direction of the Holy Ones [Godhead] on high. They have "belonged to this earth" in their time and station and are so numbered and recognized.[7]

## SUMMATION

This masterful article explains in detail various angels who have appeared to mortals on this earth. The word *angel* is applied to different classes of beings. (1) Some are spirits who have not yet been born on earth. They are premortal spirits. (2) Others are personages who have lived on the earth, but have not yet been resurrected. They are called the spirits of just men [or women] made perfect. (3) Translated beings. They are individuals who have special bodies, waiting to be changed into a resurrected being. (4) There are those who are "fallen angels." They are the third of the host of heaven who followed Lucifer or Satan, never to have the privilege of receiving a physical body. (5) A class of individuals who have gone through this earth experience and have been resurrected. They are righteous individuals who have had their spirit and body reunited, never to be separated again.

As was presented in chapter three, it is written, "the *spirit of man* in the likeness of his person" (D&C 77:2). In various scriptures, the words "*angel*," "*beings*," "*personages*," "*spirit of man*" and "*spirits*" are used and at times are written in the same sentence. These words are correctly used interchangeably in the standard works. The scriptures that were first referenced in this article illustrate this fact:

> There are two kinds of *beings* in heaven, namely: *Angels*, who are resurrected *personages*, having bodies of flesh and bones—
>
> For instance, Jesus said: Handle me and see, for a *spirit* hath not flesh and bones, as ye see me have.
>
> Secondly: the *spirits* of just men made perfect, they who are not resurrected. (D&C 129:1–3; underlines added)

Even in the quoted article, interchangeable words are correctly used in the same sentence. Concerning Lucifer or Satan, it is written: "That great *spiritual personage* was an *angel* of God in his 'first estate.'"[8] It is also apparent in this article that the duties of these classes of angels of God are varied.

As set forth in the scriptures, angels might, for example, announce the truths of the restored gospel of Jesus Christ, or convey special messages to individuals or a great body of people. They might act as guardians to protect the righteous, or to inflict divine penalties upon the wicked. At the beginning of a dispensation, they might come with authority to bestow the priesthood of God or to help in the organization of the true Church. As a ministering spirit, they go and do as they are commissioned by the Lord. In this dispensation of time, angels or spirit personages have appeared to mortals for a variety of reasons.

## Heavenly Beings Visit Joseph Smith

Many heavenly messengers appeared to the Prophet Joseph Smith after he saw and conversed with God the Father and His Son, Jesus Christ, in 1820 (Joseph Smith—History 1:15–20). As the head of the dispensation of the fulness of times, it was necessary that he receive every key, power, and authority that was given from heaven for the eternal salvation and exaltation of mankind (see D&C 110:10–16). All of the dispensations of the past had to be linked with this final great dispensation. This was accomplished by heavenly messengers from past dispensations who bestowed keys and authority upon the Prophet Joseph Smith. Besides these heads from past dispensations appearing to the Lord's chosen servant, many heavenly tutors visited Joseph Smith. In 1875, President John Taylor, then a member of the Quorum of the Twelve Apostles, said:

> And when Joseph Smith was raised up as a prophet of God, *Mormon, Moroni, Nephi* and *others of the ancient Prophets* who formerly lived on this [American] Continent, and *Peter and John* and others who lived on the Asiatic Continent, came to him and communicated to him certain principles pertaining to the Gospel of the Son of God. Why? *Because they held the keys of the various dispensations, and conferred them upon him, and he upon us [as members of the Twelve Apostles]*[9]

In 1879, President John Taylor, then President of the Quorum of the Twelve Apostles, revealed this knowledge:

> *I know of what I speak for I was very well acquainted with [the Prophet Joseph Smith] and was with him a great deal during his life, and was with him when he died.* The principles which he had, placed him in communication with the Lord, and not only with the Lord, but with the ancient apostles and prophets; such men, for instance, as *Abraham, Isaac, Jacob, Noah, Adam, Seth, Enoch, and Jesus and the Father, and the apostles that lived on this continent as well as those who lived on the Asiatic continent.* He seemed to be as familiar with these people as we are with one

another. Why? *Because he had to introduce a dispensation which was called the dispensation of the fulness of times, and it was known as such by the ancient servants of God.*[10]

Speaking of the years Joseph Smith waited to receive the plates from Moroni, Elder Orson Pratt said:

> I will state, however, that *during these four years he was often ministered to by the angels of God*, and received instruction concerning the work that was to be performed in the latter days.[11]

This statement is verified in the letter written by the Prophet Joseph Smith to "Mr. John Wentworth, Editor and Proprietor of the *Chicago Democrat*." In the Wentworth Letter, he wrote:

> The angel [Moroni] appeared to me three times the same night and unfolded the same things. *After having received many visits from the angels of God . . .* on [22 September, 1827] the angel of the Lord delivered the records into my hands.[12]

## PERSONAGES SEEN BY JOSEPH SMITH

Regarding the statement made by the Prophet of "having received many visits from the angels of God," the numbers of personages who appeared to him personally or were seen by him in vision are not entirely known. However, a significant number are documented. The following references are abbreviated: (1) Joseph Smith—History: JSH; (2) *History of The Church of Jesus Christ of Latter-day Saints*: HC; (3) Doctrine and Covenants: D&C; (4) *Teachings of the Prophet Joseph Smith*: TPJS. (5) *Journal of Discourses*: JD. The following list of personages seen by the Prophet Joseph Smith was compiled by Brother H. Donl Peterson:

1. God the Father—JSH 1:17; HC 1:5; D&C 76:20
2. Jesus Christ—JSH 1:17; HC 1:5–6; D&C 76:20–24; D&C 110:2–10

3. Moroni—JSH 1:30–49; JD 17:374
4. Elijah—D&C 110:13–16; JD 23:48
5. John the Baptist—D&C 13; HC 1:39–40
6–8. Peter, James, John—D&C 27:12; D&C 128:20; HC 1:40–42; JD 9:376; 18:326
9. Adam (Michael)—HC 2:380; 3:388; D&C 128:21; JD 18:326
10. Noah (Gabriel)—D&C 128:21; JD 21:94
11. Raphael—D&C 128:21
12. Moses—D&C 110:11; JD 21:65
13. Elias—D&C 110:12; 27:6; JD 23:48
14. Joseph, son of Jacob—D&C 27:10
15–17. Abraham, Isaac, Jacob—D&C 27:10; JD 21:94
18. Enoch—JD 21:65
19–27. 12 Jewish Apostles—JD 21:94
28–39. 12 Nephite Apostles—JD 21:94; 3 Nephi 19:4
40. Nephi—JD 21:161
41–44. Seth, Methuselah, Enos, Mahalaleel—JD 21:94; HC 3:388; D&C 107:53–57
45. Jared (Bible) HC 3:388; D&C 107:53–57
46. Lamech—JD 18:235
47. Abel—JD 18:325; HC 3:388
48. Cainan—HC 3:388; D&C 107:53–57
49. Zelph the Lamanite—HC 2:79; *Times and Seasons* 6:788
50. Alvin Smith—D&C 137; HC 2:380
51. Mormon—JD 17:374
52. Paul—TPJS 180
53. Eve—Oliver B. Huntington Diary, Part 2:214 (Located in L. Tom Perry Special Collections, Harold B. Lee Library, Brigham Young University, Provo, Utah)
54. Alma—JD 13:47
55. Unnamed angel—as to wine in sacrament; D&C 27; HC 1:106

56. Unnamed angel—sent to accept dedication of temple (*Life of Heber C. Kimball*, 106)
57. Unnamed angel—commanded polygamy, JD 20:28–29; Eliza R. Snow, biography and family records of Lorenzo Snow, 69–70
58. Many angels—Wentworth Letter, HC 4:537
59. Satan, as an angel of light—D&C 128:20; JD 3:229–30[13]

In addition to these personages who either personally visited the Prophet or were seen by him in vision, it is important to remember, and this being previously stated in chapter eight, that the Apostle Paul had a spiritual experience where he was "caught up to the third heaven." Paul also said, "He was caught up into paradise, and heard unspeakable words, which it is not lawful for a man to utter" (2 Corinthians 12:2, 4).

Concerning Paul's spiritual experience, the Prophet Joseph Smith spoke these short but meaningful words: "Paul saw the third heavens, *and I more.*"[14] Therefore, it is highly reasonable to believe that this great Latter-day Seer saw numerous personages in the celestial kingdom and in the spirit world. These would include premortal spirits and spirits in paradise and spirit prison.

## CONCLUSION

Therefore, the Prophet Joseph Smith either saw in person or by a vision the following classes of angels or personages:

(1) Gods—Godhead members.

(2) Spirits who have not yet been born on earth.

(3) Spirits in paradise and in spirit prison.

(4) Just men or women who have lived on this earth, but have not yet been resurrected.

(5) Translated beings; those personages who have special bodies, waiting to be changed into a resurrected being.

(6) Fallen Angels—Satan and his followers. They are the

third of the host of heaven who followed Lucifer or Satan, never to receive a physical body.

(7) Resurrected personages. They are a class of individuals who have sojourned here on earth, died physically, and who are now resurrected beings.

Truly, Joseph Smith was a choice prophet, seer, and revelator (see D&C 21:1; 107:92). The countless personal manifestations he received from various classes of angels and personages mentioned throughout the scriptures were spiritual gifts of inestimable worth.

## NOTES

1. "Who and What are the Angels?" *Improvement Era*, edited by Joseph F. Smith and Edward H. Anderson, August 1912, No. 10, 949–50; emphasis added.
2. Ibid., 950; emphasis added.
3. Ibid.; emphasis added.
4. Ibid., 951; emphasis added. The Prophet Joseph Smith also said "An Angel of God never has wings," Joseph Smith, *Teachings of the Prophet Joseph Smith*, selected by Joseph Fielding Smith (Salt Lake City: Deseret Book, 1976), 162; emphasis added. See also Joseph Smith, *History of The Church of Jesus Christ of Latter-day Saints*, 7 vols., edited by B. H. Roberts (Salt Lake City: Deseret Book, 1976), 3:392.
5. Ibid.; emphasis added.
6. Ibid.
7. Ibid., 951–52; emphasis added.
8. Ibid., 951; emphasis added.
9. John Taylor, *Journal of Discourses*, 26 vols. (London: Latter-day Saints Book Depot, 1854–86), 17:374–75; emphasis added.
10. Taylor, *Journal of Discourses*, 21:94; emphasis added.

11. Orson Pratt, *Journal of Discourses*, 15:185; emphasis added.

12. Smith, *History of The Church*, 4:537.

13. List and references compiled by H. Donl Peterson, quoted in Brian L. Smith's "Joseph Smith: Gifted Learner, Master Teacher, Prophetic Seer" (Provo, Utah: Brigham Young University Religious Studies Center, 1993), 169–81. See also W. Jeffrey Marsh, *The Eyewitness History of the Church* (Springville, Utah: Cedar Fort, 2005), 128–29.

14. Smith, *Teachings of the Prophet Joseph Smith*, 301; emphasis added. See also Smith, *History of the Church*, 5:392.

## CHAPTER 11

# PROGRESSION IN THE SPIRIT WORLD

## INFORMATIVE STATEMENTS

As was explained in chapter nine, there are various subdivisions in the spirit world with their corresponding levels of advancement. In a Church publication, Elder Charles W. Penrose wrote a significant description of the spirit world:

> There are conditions of spirit life between death and the resurrection. There are *two grand divisions* in the spirit world; the good gravitate to and associate with the good; the bad with the bad. *There are doubtless many subdivisions in each of these spirit spheres*, according to the various grades and qualities of the individuals and their course of life when in the body. *They are capable of receiving information, can exercise faith, repentance and obedience, or take an opposite course.* Volition, or will power, is an attribute of the spirit of man, and that is why he is responsible for his conduct whether in the body or out of the body, and why, therefore, he will be brought to judgment, and his eternal status will be "according to his works."
>
> The portion of the spirit world where the good dwell between death and the resurrection, is sometimes called *paradise*, and that where the evil abide is called hades, or *hell*.[1]

In harmony with this statement, President Brigham Young said this of the spirit world:

We have no time to spend foolishly, for we have just as much on our hands as we can probably do, to keep pace with that portion of our brethren who have gone into the other room.

*And when we have passed into the sphere where Joseph [Smith] is, there is still another department, and then another, and another, and so on to an eternal progression in exaltation and eternal lives. That is the exaltation I am looking for.*[2]

This statement is supported by the comment made by President Heber C. Kimball at the funeral services of President Jedediah M. Grant when he said:

> He asked his wife Caroline [in the spirit world] where Joseph and Hyrum and Father Smith and others were; she replied, "*they have gone away ahead, to perform and transact business for us.*" The same as when brother Brigham and his brethren left Winter Quarters [on earth] and came here [in the west] to search out a home; they came to find a location for their brethren.[3]

As was written in chapter three, President Woodruff, then a member of the Quorum of the Twelve Apostles, said that "during my travels in the southern country last winter I had *many interviews with President [Brigham] Young, and with Heber C. Kimball, and Geo. A. Smith, and Jedediah M. Grant, and many others who are dead.*"[4]

While speaking with President Brigham Young, who was dead, President Woodruff told of an impression that came to him:

> The thought came to me that Brother Joseph [Smith] had left the work of watching over this church and kingdom to others, and that he had gone ahead, and that he had left this work to men who have lived and labored with us since he left us. This idea manifested itself to me, *that such men advance in the spirit world.*[5]

These statements verify that righteous individuals are allowed to progress to a higher sphere or level in the spirit world. Those individuals have to perfect themselves to a level where they are eligible to dwell there. This is supported by what President Brigham Young said:

> And when we have passed into the sphere where Joseph [Smith] is, there is still another department, and then another, and another, and so on to an eternal progression in exaltation and eternal lives. That is the exaltation I am looking for.[6]

## THE CHURCH IS ORGANIZED IN THE SPIRIT WORLD

It is the belief of members of The Church of Jesus Christ of Latter-day Saints that gospel instruction and advancement in the spirit world is under the direction of our Savior, Jesus Christ. This statement is supported by the vision of the redemption of the dead as seen by President Joseph F. Smith. Said he:

> While this vast multitude waited and conversed, rejoicing in the hour of their deliverance from the chains of death, *the Son of God appeared*, declaring liberty to the captives who had been faithful; And there he preached to them the everlasting gospel . . .
> *But his ministry among those who were dead was limited to the brief time intervening between the crucifixion and his resurrection . . .*
> *But behold, from among the righteous, he organized his forces and appointed messengers, clothed with power and authority, and commissioned them to go forth and carry the light of the gospel to them that were in darkness, even to all the spirits of men; and thus was the gospel preached to the dead.*" (D&C 138:18–19, 27, 30; emphasis added)

This supports the belief that the Church is in full operation in this realm. Therefore, when a faithful priesthood holder passes from mortality, he continues with his duties and responsibilities in the spirit world as he did in mortality. Providing additional information, President Brigham Young taught this doctrine:

> *When the faithful Elders, holding this Priesthood, go into the spirit world they carry with them the same power and Priesthood that they had while in the mortal tabernacle."*[7]

In harmony with this teaching, President Wilford Woodruff, then President of the Quorum of the Twelve Apostles, revealed this knowledge:

> *The same Priesthood exists on the other side of the veil.* Every man who is faithful in his quorum here will join his quorum there. When a man dies and his body is laid in the tomb [grave], he does not lose his position . . . and *every Apostle, every Seventy, every Elder, etc., who has died in the faith as soon as he passes to the other side of the veil, enters into the work of the ministry,* and there is a thousand times more to preach there than there is here.[8]

President Brigham Young taught that those who have the priesthood are allowed to labor more effectively in the spirit world. Said he:

> Much has been said about the power of the Latter-day Saints. Is it the people called Latter-day Saints that have this power, or is it the Priesthood? *It is the Priesthood*; and if they live according to that Priesthood, they can commence their work here and gain many victories, and be prepared to receive glory, immortality, and eternal life, *that when they go into the spirit-world, their work will far surpass that of any other man or being that has not been blessed with the keys of the Priesthood here [in mortality].*[9]

According to the Prophet Joseph Smith, the Church is organized in the spirit world according to the dispensations in which men lived in mortality, with the prophet who was responsible for each generation to preside at the head of the Church among those people he was responsible for. Concerning this teaching, the Prophet said:

> *This then, is the nature of the Priesthood; every man holding the Presidency of his dispensation,* and one man holding the

Presidency of them all, even Adam; and Adam receiving his Presidency and authority from the Lord, but cannot receive a fullness until Christ shall present the Kingdom to the Father, which shall be at the end of the last dispensation.[10]

President Brigham Young revealed this knowledge about the Prophet Joseph Smith:

> *Joseph Smith holds the keys of this last dispensation, and is now engaged behind the veil in the great work of the last days* . . . He holds the keys of that kingdom for the last dispensation— the keys to rule in the spirit-world; and he rules there trium- phantly, . . . *and he will never cease his operations, under the direc- tions of the Son of God, until the last ones of the children of men are saved that can be, from Adam till now.*[11]

In total harmony with this teaching, President Wilford Woodruff also said this about the Prophet:

> The Prophet Joseph Smith held the keys of this dispensa- tion on this side of the veil, and he will hold them throughout the countless ages of eternity. He went into the spirit world to unlock the prison doors and to preach the Gospel to the millions of spirits who are in darkness.[12]

## AGENCY TO ACCEPT THE GOSPEL

The crucified Son of God appeared in paradise, "declaring liberty to the captives who had been faithful. . . . From among the righteous, he organized his forces and appointed messen- gers, clothed with power and authority, and commissioned them to go forth and carry the light of the gospel to them that were in darkness, even to all the spirits of men; and thus was the gospel preached to the dead." President Smith further saw that the "dead who repent will be redeemed, through obedience to the ordinances of the house of God, and after they have paid the penalty of their transgressions, and are washed clean, shall receive a reward according to their works, for they are heirs of salvation" (see D&C 138:18, 30, 58–59).

Accordingly, the gospel is preached to a multitude of spirits in that part of the spirit world called spirit prison. With agency in full force, these spirits can either accept or reject the gospel message. This is made evident in an address given by President James E. Faust, then an Assistant to the Quorum of the Twelve Apostles:

> My wife's mother's twin sister died a few weeks ago and a few days before she passed away, she came down to breakfast and told her family, she being quite aged, that, "You're not going to believe this, but last night Jim (meaning her brother Jim Hamilton, former bishop out in Lincoln Ward and the patriarch of the Granite Stake until last year when he passed away) came to me last night and told me that my time was coming, that he'd be back for me in just a few days and that I should get ready and tell you all. And then she said that mother was lonesome and missed her daughters," and then made a very significant statement. She said that *"Bishop Hamilton said the people on the other side, some of them have a hard time [listening] to the message of the gospel."*[13]

The Lord's chosen servants have made statements to indicate that thousands—and it is hoped millions or even billions—could embrace the gospel in the spirit world. Again, with agency in full force, and without many of the false teachings, improper traditions, and the temptations of mortality—all of which can deter individuals from embracing the truth—might be eliminated so that individuals can hear the gospel of Jesus Christ preached by those righteous spirits commissioned to carry the gospel message to the dead (see D&C 138:30, 57–58).

President Wilford Woodruff revealed this knowledge:

> Great and glorious are these principles which God has revealed to us concerning the redemption of our dead. I tell you when the prophets and apostles go to preach to those who are shut up in prison, and who have not received the gospel, *thousands of them will there embrace the gospel.* They know more in that world than they do here.[14]

## CONCLUSION

Recalling previous statements verifying that righteous individuals are allowed to progress to higher spheres or levels in the spirit world, it is important to emphasize that these individuals are required to perfect themselves to such an extent that they are deemed fit to dwell in these progressively higher states. This is supported by what President Brigham Young said:

> And when we have passed into the sphere where Joseph [Smith] is, there is still another department, and then another, and another, and so on to an eternal progression in exaltation and eternal lives. That is the exaltation I am looking for.[15]

## NOTES

1. Charles W. Penrose, *The Millennial Star*, March 14, 1907, 69:168–69; emphasis added. See also *Journal of Discourses*, 26 vols. (London: Latter-day Saints Book Depot, 1854–86), 23:161.
2. Brigham Young, *Journal of Discourses*, 3:375; emphasis added.
3. Heber C. Kimball, funeral services of Jedediah M. Grant, Dec. 4, 1856. See *Journal of Discourses*, 4:136; emphasis added.
4. Wilford Woodruff, *Journal of Discourses*, 21:318; emphasis added.
5. Ibid.; emphasis added.
6. Young, *Journal of Discourses*, 3:375.
7. Young, *Journal of Discourses*, 3:371; emphasis added.
8. Woodruff, *Journal of Discourses*, 22:333–34; emphasis added. The word *vail* has been modernized to *veil*.
9. Young, *Journal of Discourses*, 7:288–89; emphasis added.
10. Joseph Smith, *Teachings of the Prophet Joseph Smith*, selected by Joseph Fielding Smith (Salt Lake City: Deseret Book, 1976), 169; emphasis added.

11. Young, *Journal of Discourses*, 7:289; emphasis added. The word *vail* has been modernized to *veil*.

12. Woodruff, *Journal of Discourses*, 22:333–34. The word *vail* has been modernized to *veil*.

13. James E. Faust, Regional Representatives Seminar, October 5, 1972, p. 1 (38).

14. Wilford Woodruff, *The Discourses of Wilford Woodruff*, selected by G. Homer Durham (Salt Lake City: Bookcraft, 1969), 152.

15. Young, *Journal of Discourses*, 3:375.

## CHAPTER 12

# HEAVENLY MANIFESTATIONS

## ENTRY INTO THE SPIRIT WORLD IS PLEASANT

When mortal death occurs, it immediately provides a relief from the physical difficulties and trials of mortality. This statement is supported by a statement recorded in the Book of Mormon. Specifically speaking of individuals who are worthy to reside in that part of the spirit world called paradise, Alma revealed this knowledge:

> The spirits of those who are righteous are received into a state of happiness, which is called paradise, a state of rest, a state of peace, where they shall rest from all their troubles and from all care, and sorrow. (Alma 40:12)

In total harmony with this scripture, President Brigham Young spoke these comforting and uplifting words:

> We shall turn round and look upon it [the valley of death] and think, when we have crossed it, why this is the greatest advantage of my whole existence, *for I have passed from a state of sorrow, grief, mourning, woe, misery, pain, anguish and disappointment into a state of existence, where I can enjoy life to the fullest extent as far as that can be done without a body. My spirit is set free, I thirst no more, I want to sleep no more, I hunger no more, I tire no more, I run, I walk, I labor, I go, I come, I do this, I do that,*

*whatever is required of me, nothing like pain or weariness, I am full of life, full of vigor,* and I enjoy the presence of my heavenly Father, by the power of His Spirit."[1]

President Francis M. Lyman, then President of the Quorum of the Twelve Apostles, spoke these assuring words:

> It will be all right when our time comes, when we have finished our work and accomplished what the Lord requires of us. If we are prepared, we need not be afraid to go, *for it will be one of the most pleasant sensations that ever comes to the soul of man,* whenever he departs, if he can go with a clear conscience into the presence of the Lord . . . . We will be full of joy and happiness, and we will enter in a place of rest, of peace, of joy, rest from every sorrow. What a blessed thing that will be! *We will never be tired any more.* We will not get tired, for we will be in a condition that we can endure and enjoy our work; for we shall be occupied and employed on the other side as we are on this side; we shall have plenty to occupy our attention right along.[2]

As was written in chapter four, it is important to emphasize that we do not seek death, though it is part of the merciful plan of God the Father. We rejoice in life, and desire to live as long as we can in mortality. *Yet, when death eventually comes, it can be peaceful and sweet.* These teachings from Alma, President Young, and Elder Lyman truly verify this *gospel truth.*

## INCREASED ABILITY OF SPIRIT PERSONAGES

Not only will death be one of the most pleasant sensations that will ever come to the soul of man, but it will also return the spirit to the full use of powers that were enjoyed during our premortal existence. Though a healthy mortal body is amazing in its functions and ability, it pales to what the mind or spirit can achieve in the post-mortal existence. Regarding the mortal body, Elder Orson Pratt said:

> *Our happiness here [on earth] is regulated in a great measure by external objects, by the organization of the mortal tabernacle;*

they are not permitted to rise very high, or to become very great; *on the other hand it seems to be a kind of limit to our joys and pleasures, sufferings, and pains, and this is because of the imperfection of the tabernacle in which we dwell*; and of those things with which we are surrounded; but in that life everything will appear in its true colors; . . . This tabernacle, although it is good in its place, is something like the scaffolding you see round about a new building that is going up; it is only a help, an aid in this imperfect situation; *but when we get into another condition [after death], we shall find that these imperfect aids will not be particularly wanted; we shall have other sources of gaining knowledge, besides these inlets, called senses.*[3]

One of the abilities that a spirit personage will realize is the capability for rapid movement from one place to another. As President Brigham Young revealed in the funeral service of Aurelia Spencer:

*The brightness and glory of the next apartment [life in the spirit world] is inexpressible.* It is not encumbered with this clog of dirt [mortal body] we are carrying around here so that when we advance in years we have to be stubbing along and to be careful lest we fall down. We see our youth, even, frequently stubbing their toes and falling down. But yonder [in the spirit world] how different! *They move with ease and like lightning.*[4]

In a funeral service of Daniel Spencer, President Brigham Young provided this knowledge:

*As quickly as the spirit is unlocked from this house of clay, it is free to travel with lightning speed to any planet, or fixed star, or to the uttermost part of the earth, or to the depths of the sea, according to the will of Him [the Lord] who dictates.*[5]

As we anticipate the time in the spirit world for rapid movement, we can expect that our senses will be expanded. Elder Orson Pratt asked this intriguing question, "How do we know, when this spirit is freed from this mortal tabernacle, but that all [of our] senses will be greatly enlarged?"[6]

He then provides this answer:

The spirit is inherently capable of experiencing the sensations of light; if it were not so, we could not see . . . Then unclothe the spirit, and instead of exposing a small portion of it about the size of a pea [pupil of the mortal eye] to the action of the rays of light, the whole of it [entire spirit body] would be exposed. *I think we could then see in different directions at once, instead of looking in one particular direction; we could then look all around us at the same instant.* . . . I believe we shall be freed, in the next world, in a great measure, from these narrow, contracted methods of thinking. *Instead of thinking in one channel, and following up one certain course of reasoning to find a certain truth, knowledge will rush in from all quarters; . . . informing the spirit, and giving understanding concerning ten thousand things at the same time; and the mind will be capable of receiving and retaining all.*[7]

In addition to tremendous retention power given a spirit, as explained by Elder Pratt, it is anticipated that we will also have the capacity to travel through time, or perhaps see things as they were in the past or will be in the future. President Brigham Young provides this intriguing insight:

*If we want to behold Jerusalem as it was in the days of the Savior; or if we want to see the Garden of Eden as it was when created, there we are, and we see it as it existed spiritually, for it was created first spiritually and then temporally, and spiritually it still remains.* And when there we may behold the earth as at the dawn of creation, or we may visit any city we please that exists upon its [the earth's] surface.[8]

This statement is supported by what is written in the scriptures. Moses, for one, "beheld the world and the ends thereof, and all the children of men which are, and which were created" (Moses 1:8). He then explains that he saw all of this with his own eyes, "but not my natural, *but my spiritual eyes*, for my natural eyes could not have beheld" (Moses 1:11; emphasis added). The vision shown to Enoch, who saw "all things, even unto the end of the world" (Moses 7:67) must have been received in like manner.

As written in the Book of Mormon, the brother of Jared was shown both the past and the future with his spiritual eyes as he conversed with the premortal Lord on mount Shelem. The scripture states that "the veil was taken from off the eyes of the brother of Jared . . ." and that "he could not be kept from beholding within the veil," therefore the Lord "*showed unto the brother of Jared all the inhabitants of the earth which had been, and also all that would be; and he withheld them not from his sight, even unto the ends of the earth*" (Ether 3:6, 19, 25; emphasis added).

President Heber C. Kimball, then First Counselor in the First Presidency, also spoke of the power of increased sight while telling of a vision of evil spirits that he saw while serving a mission in England:

> All at once my vision was opened, *and the walls of the building were no obstruction to my seeing, for I saw nothing but the visions that presented themselves.* Why did not the walls obstruct my view? Because my spirit could look through the walls of that house, *for I looked with that spirit, element, and power, with which angels look; and as God sees all things,* so were invisible things brought before me, *as the Lord would bring things before Joseph [Smith] in the Urim and Thummim. It was upon that principle that the Lord showed things to the Prophet Joseph.*[9]

For righteous spirits who are partially judged to reside in paradise, they can look forward to regaining many powers that have been limited during their mortal state of existence. These statements by the Lord's chosen servants adequately describe the increased ability of spirit personages.

## CLOTHING IN THE SPIRIT WORLD

In 1882, President John Taylor revealed this knowledge about death:

When we go to the spirit world, *we go naked*, as we came into the world, or *if we get any clothing it is as much by our dependence upon others as when we were born into this world*. If we get a mansion in our Father's Kingdom we shall also be dependent upon Him for it.[10]

The clothing that spirits and resurrected personages wear is described in different ways. In a dream vision, Daniel was able to see Adam, the first man on this earth, described as the "Ancient of days," sitting, "*whose garment was white as snow*" (Daniel 7:9; emphasis added). John the Revelator described the dress of the righteous martyrs slain for the testimony of our Lord, saying that, "*white robes were given unto every one of them*" (Revelation 6:9–11; emphasis added). In Lehi's vision of the tree of life, he says "I saw a man, and he was *dressed in a white robe*; and he came and stood before me. And it came to pass that he spake unto me, and bade me follow him" (1 Nephi 8:5–6; emphasis added). After Jesus Christ had been crucified and his deceased body had been laid in a borrowed tomb, it is written that "Mary stood without at the sepulcher weeping: and as she wept, she stooped down, and looked into the sepulcher, And seeth *two angels in white* sitting, the one at the head, and the other at the feet, where the body of Jesus had lain" (John 20:11–12; emphasis added).

The Prophet Joseph Smith gave a detailed description of the clothing worn by the Angel Moroni:

> *He had on a loose robe of most exquisite whiteness*. It was a whiteness beyond anything earthly I had ever seen; nor do I believe that any earthly thing could be made to appear so exceedingly white and brilliant. His hands were naked, and his arms also, a little above the wrist; so, also, were his feet naked, as were his legs, a little above the ankles. His head and neck were also bare. I could discover that he had no other clothing on but this robe, as it was open, so that I could see into his bosom. (Joseph Smith—History 1:31; emphasis added)

On March 15, 1848, President Wilford Woodruff, then a member of the Quorum of the Twelve Apostles, described the following scenes he saw in a "remarkable dream in which he passed in spirit through the air from state to state, escaped from his enemies and passed on to heaven."

"I saw," he says, "Joseph and Hyrum [Smith] and many others of the Latter-day Saints who had died. The innumerable company of souls which I saw seemed to be preparing for some grand and important event which I could not understand. Many were engaged in making crowns for the Saints. *They were all dressed in white robes, both male and female.*"[11]

As was written in chapter three, President Woodruff said:

> But during my travels in the southern country last winter I had *many interviews with President [Brigham] Young, and with Heber C. Kimball, and Geo. A. Smith, and Jedediah M. Grant, and many others who are dead* . . .
>
> I saw Brother Brigham and Brother Heber ride in carriage ahead of the carriage in which I rode when I was on my way to attend conference; *and they were dressed in the most priestly robes.*[12]

Elder Alonzo A. Hinckley, a member of the Quorum of the Twelve Apostles, was visited by three visitors from beyond the veil dressed in temple robes.

> Shortly before Elder Hinckley's death [Dec. 22, 1936, at age 66[13]], his daughter, Afton, was with him in his home in Salt Lake City. The family had gone out. Everything was quiet, there was an indescribably sweet influence in the house. She supposed her father was asleep and after some little time she went to his room. When she appeared at the door, he said, "Come in, I have had a wonderful afternoon. *Three heavenly messengers dressed in the robes of the Holy Priesthood have been my visitors.*" He spoke of them teaching him to sing a hymn. At that juncture, the family began to appear and he never mentioned the matter again.[14]

Mary Ellen Jensen, whose nickname was "Ella," suffered

from scarlet fever for several weeks. This young woman of fifteen years of age was dead for three and a half hours. Through the priesthood administration of President Lorenzo Snow, then President of the Quorum of the Twelve Apostles, along with Brother Rudger Clawson, then stake president in Brigham City, Utah, Ella returned to life on March 3, 1891. While Sister Jensen was in the spirit world, she met deceased relatives. Relating things she saw and heard in the spirit world, Sister Jensen spoke of the clothing worn by individuals in this realm:

> The people were all dressed in white or cream, excepting Uncle Hans Jensen, who had on his dark clothes and long rubber boots, the things he wore when he was drowned in the Snake River in Idaho.[15]

Ella's description of her deceased uncle illustrates that at various times "when the dead manifest themselves to the living they usually appear as they were last seen on earth so that the living will recognize them."[16]

From the descriptions presented, a *majority* of mortals on earth who are visited by either spirits from paradise or resurrected beings *generally* describe the clothing worn by these heavenly personages *as being a robe and being white in color.*

## LANDSCAPE IN PARADISE

In one of his many published writings, President Joseph Fielding Smith, then President of the Quorum of the Twelve Apostles, wrote the following description:

> Since all creatures and the *plants and trees of the earth were created spiritually*, we discover that not only man is entitled to the resurrection but every other living thing that suffered the fall through Adam's transgression.[17]

As "plants and trees of the earth were created spiritually" and will eventually be resurrected, it would be natural that similar foliage would be seen in the spirit world. A statement made by

President Brigham Young supports this. During his remarks, he spoke these informative words:

> When the [last] breath leaves the [mortal] body, your life has not become extinct; your life is still in existence. And when you are in the spirit world, *everything there will appear as natural as things now do [on earth].*[18]

Some of the things that will "appear as natural as things now do" are a variety of landscapes in the spirit world. Individuals who have been permitted to visit this realm and return again to mortality have made various descriptions of landscapes. It is important to emphasize that the following statements are only describing portions or areas of the spirit world that were viewed.

As was written in chapter nine, President Heber C. Kimball, then First Counselor in the First Presidency, speaking at the funeral of President Jedediah M. Grant, who was Second Counselor in the First Presidency, said:

> He [a dying President Grant] said to me, "brother Heber, I have been into the spirit world two nights in succession."[19] President Grant then told of the *beautiful flowers he saw* while visiting paradise: "I have seen *good gardens* on this earth, *but I never saw any to compare with those that were there. I saw flowers of numerous kinds,* and some with from *fifty to a hundred different colored flowers growing upon one stalk.*"[20]

In this same funeral sermon, President Heber C. Kimball said that:

> . . . brother Grant said that *he felt extremely sorrowful at having to leave so beautiful a place* and come back to earth, for he looked upon his body with loathing, but was obliged to enter it again.[21]

Due to his physical frailty, President George Albert Smith, then a member of the Quorum of the Twelve Apostles, traveled with his family to St. George, Utah, in 1909, to help in the recovery of his health. While in this location, President Smith lost consciousness and thought he had passed to the spirit world. While in the spirit world, he described the landscape of an area he viewed:

> I found myself standing with my back to *a large and beautiful lake*, facing a *great forest of trees*. There was no one in sight, and there was no boat upon the lake or any other visible means to indicate how I might have arrived there. I realized, or seemed to realize, that I had finished my work in mortality and had gone home. I began to look around, to see if I could not find someone. There was no evidence of anyone living there, just those *great, beautiful trees* in front of me and the *wonderful lake* behind me.
>
> I began to explore, and soon I found a *trail through the woods* which seemed to have been used very little, and which was *almost obscured by grass*. I followed this *trail*, and after I had walked for some time and traveled a considerable distance through the forest, I saw a man coming towards me [who was my grandfather, George A. Smith].[22]

It is believed by some that in the central part of the spirit world is a significant tree. As revealed by John the Revelator, the tree of life stands "in the midst of the paradise of God" (Revelation 2:7). While it is true that the tree of life that Lehi and Nephi saw in vision is interpreted to mean the love of God (see 1 Nephi 11:21–22), Nephi provides a vivid description of this significant tree. He said its "beauty thereof was far beyond, yea, exceeding of all beauty; and the whiteness thereof did exceed the whiteness of the driven snow" (1 Nephi 11:8). Concerning those who die and are partially judged to go into that part of the spirit world called spirit prison and those who go into paradise, this same Nephi revealed this knowledge:

> Wherefore, the wicked are rejected from the righteous, and also from that *tree of life*, whose fruit is most precious and most desirable above all other fruits; yea, and it is the greatest of all the gifts of God. (1 Nephi 15:36; emphasis added)

These quoted statements provide ample substantiation that there are a variety of landscapes in the spirit world. Repeating again what President Brigham Young stated: "And when you are in the spirit world, *everything there will appear as natural as things now do [on earth].*"[23]

## BUILDINGS IN PARADISE

Concerning buildings that are in the spirit world, President Heber C. Kimball, in explaining what President Jedediah M. Grant saw, said:

> He also spoke of the buildings he saw there, remarking that the Lord gave Solomon wisdom and poured gold and silver into his hands that he might display his skill and ability, and said that *the temple erected by Solomon was much inferior to the most ordinary buildings he saw in the spirit world.*[24]

Brother Orson F. Whitney (who several years later would be ordained a member of the Quorum of the Twelve Apostles[25]), wrote of the experiences of David P. Kimball, the fourth son of President Heber C. Kimball (of the First Presidency, who died June 22, 1868[26]). David had a number of visions and manifestations during a week in November 1881 when he was lost and without food or water on the Salt River desert in Arizona. David saw in vision deceased members of the Church who were in that part of the spirit world called paradise.

> I was then taken in the vision into a *vast building, which was built on the plan of the Order of Zion.* I entered through a south door and found myself in a part of the building which was unfinished, though a great many workmen were busy upon it. My guide showed me all through this half of the house, and then took me through the other half, which was finished. *The richness, grandeur and beauty of it defied description. There were many apartments in the house, which was very spacious, and they differed in size and the fineness of the workmanship, according to the merits on earth of those who were to occupy them.* I felt most

at home in the unfinished part, among the workmen. *The upper part of the house was filled with Saints,* but I could not see them, though some of them conversed with me, my father and mother, Uncle Joseph Young and others.[27]

Ella Jensen, who was in the spirit world for three and a half hours, returned to life by the administration of President Lorenzo Snow and Brother Rudger Clawson, gave this description of what she saw:

> As soon as I had a glimpse of the other world *I was anxious to go and all the care and worry left me.*
>
> *I entered a large hall.* It was so long that I could not see the end of it. It was filled with people. . . . I passed on through the room and met a great many of my relatives and friends. It was like going along the crowded streets of a city where you meet many people, only a very few of whom you recognize. . . . *Everybody appeared to be perfectly happy.* I was having a very pleasant visit with each one that I knew. Finally I reached the end of that long room. I opened a door and went into another room.[28]

As was written in chapter three, President Wilford Woodruff said:

> Joseph Smith [the Prophet] continued visiting myself and others up to a certain time, and then it stopped. The last time I saw him was in heaven. *In the night vision I saw him at the door of the temple in heaven.* He came to me and spoke to me.[29]

This statement verifies that there is a temple in heaven [probably meaning paradise]. Though the dead have work done for them vicariously on earth by mortals in the temples on earth, it is reasonable to believe that there is a sacred edifice in that part of the spirit world where the righteous spirits reside.

Seven months before he passed away, President Joseph F. Smith recorded a dream he had while he was serving a mission when he was young. In this dream he was on a journey, and he felt impressed to hurry for fear that he might be late. In his words, he said that "I came *to a wonderful mansion*, if it could be called a mansion. It seemed too large, too great to have been made by hand, but I thought I knew that was my destination." He then said that he saw "a notice, 'Bath.'" He quickly went and bathed and opened up a bundle and there "was a pair of white, clean garments." He put them on and rushed to a great door. He said,

> I knocked and the door opened, and the man who stood there was the Prophet Joseph Smith. He looked at me a little reprovingly, and the first words he said: "Joseph, you are late." Yet I took confidence and said:
> "Yes, but I am clean—I am clean!"
> He clasped my hand and drew me in, then closed the great door. I felt his hand just as tangible as I ever felt the hand of man. I knew him, and when I entered I saw my father, and Brigham and Heber, and Willard, and other good men that I had known, standing in a row.[30]

Evidently, in this dream vision, Joseph F. Smith saw and spoke with the Prophet Joseph Smith at the door of a "wonderful mansion" in the spirit world. Therefore, these quoted statements adequately describe a few of the items that are in that part of the spirit world called paradise.

## CONCLUSION

The spirit world is a temporary home for the spirits of mankind. It is a place of learning, of waiting for the spirit and the body to be reunited, of peace and rest, and of instruction and preparation for the final judgment of our Lord and Savior. Some of the spirits in the spirit world are allowed to visit mortals on earth and give them counsel and instruction. Some mortals are allowed to visit with spirits who reside in the spirit world. Therefore, heavenly manifestations provide a means whereby the Lord blesses and instructs His children who are assigned to this earth. The greatest accomplishment of both the Father and the Son consists in bringing to pass the immortality and eternal life of man (see Moses 1:39). Our hope for eternal happiness is to find and stay on the straight and narrow path that leads to eternal life. Our Father wants us to succeed and to become like Him. He has provided both in this life and the life to come the way whereby we can accomplish this. The way is called the gospel of Jesus Christ. Truly, the gospel blesses the lives of those who reside on earth and in the spirit world. The gospel of Jesus Christ gives great hope that each individual can one day become like our Heavenly Father and His Son, Jesus Christ, and partake of the same happiness, glory, and eternal life that they enjoy.

------

## NOTES

1. Brigham Young, funeral services of Thomas Williams, July 19, 1874. See *Journal of Discourses*, 26 vols. (London: Latter-day Saints Book Depot, 1854–86), 17:142; emphasis added.

2. Francis M. Lyman, in Conference Report, October 3, 1909, 19; emphasis added.

3. Orson Pratt, *Journal of Discourses*, 2:240, 244; emphasis added.

4. Brigham Young, *Journal of Discourses*, 14:231; emphasis added.

5. Young, *Journal of Discourses*, 13:77; emphasis added.

6. Pratt, *Journal of Discourses*, 2:243.

7. Ibid., 243, 246; emphasis added.

8. Young, *Journal of Discourses*, 14:231; emphasis added.

9. Heber C. Kimball, *Journal of Discourses*, 4:2; emphasis added.

10. John Taylor, Logan Quarterly Conference, April 1882. See Mat-thias F. Cowley, *Wilford Woodruff*, 7th ed. (Salt Lake City: Book-craft, 1978), 541.

11. Ibid., 328.

12. Wilford Woodruff, *Journal of Discourses*, 21:318; emphasis added.

13. *Deseret News 2001–2002 Church Almanac* (Salt Lake City: Deseret News, 2002) 67.

14. Bryant S. Hinckley, *The Faith of Our Pioneer Fathers* (Salt Lake City: Deseret Book, 1959), 236. See also Duane S. Crowther, *Life Everlasting* (Salt Lake City: Bookcraft, 1972), 82.

15. LeRoi C. Snow, "Raised From the Dead," *Improvement Era*, Vol. XXXII, No. 12, October 1929, 973–74. See also Crowther, *Life Everlasting*, 6, 10–12, 81.

16. Ibid., 974.

17. Joseph Fielding Smith, *Answers to Gospel Questions*, compiled by Joseph Fielding Smith Jr., 5 vols. (Salt Lake City: Deseret Book, 1957–66), 4:130.

18. Young, *Journal of Discourses*, 7:239; emphasis added.

19. Heber C. Kimball, funeral services of Jedediah M. Grant, Dec. 4, 1856. See *Journal of Discourses*, 4:135; emphasis added.

20. Ibid., 136.

21. Ibid.

22. The following was from three works: (1) *Sharing the Gospel with Others, Excerpts from the Sermons of President Smith*, compiled by Preston Nibley (Salt Lake City: Deseret Book, 1948) 110–11; (2) Duane S. Crowther, *Life Everlasting*, 75; and (3) *The Presidents of the Church*, edited by Leonard J. Arrington (Salt Lake City: Deseret Book, 1986), 258. In this article by Merlo J. Pusey, he writes that President Smith "dreamed one night that he met his grandfather, George A. Smith, on a trail in the woods."

23. Young, *Journal of Discourses*, 7:239; emphasis added.

24. Kimball, funeral services of Jedediah M. Grant. See *Journal of Discourses*, 4:136; emphasis added.

25. *Deseret News 2001–2002 Church Almanac*, 66.

26. Ibid., 57.

27. Orson F. Whitney, "A Terrible Ordeal," *Helpful Visions*, 14th vol. in a series (Salt Lake City: Juvenile Instructor Office, 1887), 13. See also Crowther, *Life Everlasting*, 77.

28. Snow, "Raised From the Dead," 973–74. See also Crowther, *Life Everlasting*, 6.

29. Wilford Woodruff, *The Discourses of Wilford Woodruff*, selected by G. Homer Durham (Salt Lake City: Bookcraft, 1969), 288.

30. Joseph F. Smith, *Gospel Doctrine: Selections from the Sermons and Writings of Joseph F. Smith* (Salt Lake City: Deseret Book, 1971), 541–42.

# BIBLIOGRAPHY

*A Commentary on The Holy Bible* (commonly referred to as *The One-Volume Bible Commentary*). Edited by The Reverend J. R. Dummelow. 31st ed. New York: The Macmillan Company, 1970.

Cannon, George Q. *Deseret News Weekly*. No. 22, May 15, 1897. Salt Lake City: The Church of Jesus Christ of Latter-day Saints, 1850–98.

———. *The Millennial Star*. Editorial. September 14, 1891. Manchester, London, and Liverpool England: The Church of Jesus Christ of Latter-day Saints, 1840–1970.

Conference Reports of The Church of Jesus Christ of Latter-day Saints. October 1909; April 1928; April 1949; April 1963; October 1964; October 1970; October 1971. Salt Lake City: The Church of Jesus Christ of Latter-day Saints, 1898 to present.

Cowley, Matthias F. *Wilford Woodruff, History of His Life and Labors*. Salt Lake City: Bookcraft, 1978.

Crowther, Duane S. *Life Everlasting*. Salt Lake City: Bookcraft, 1972.

*Deseret News 2001–2002 Church Almanac*. Salt Lake City: Deseret News, 2002.

Dyer, Alvin R. *Who Am I?* Salt Lake City: Deseret Book, 1963.

Faust, James E. Regional Representatives Seminary Address. October 5, 1972.

Hinckley, Bryant S. *The Faith of Our Pioneer Fathers*. Salt Lake City: Deseret Book, 1959.

_____. *Sermons and Missionary Services of Melvin Joseph Ballard*. 18th ed. Salt Lake City: Deseret Book, 1973.

*Improvement Era*. Edited by Joseph F. Smith and Edward H. Anderson. Vol. XV, No. 10, August 1912. Salt Lake City, Utah: The Church of Jesus Christ of Latter-day Saints, 1897–70.

*Journal of Discourses*. 26 vols. London: Latter-day Saints Book Depot, 1854–86.

Kenney, Scott. "Joseph F. Smith." *The Presidents of the Church: Biographical Essays*. Edited by Leonard J. Arrington. Salt Lake City: Deseret Book, 1986.

Lee, Harold B. "Be Loyal to the Royal Within You." Brigham Young University stake conference address. Provo, Utah. October 20, 1957.

_____. "Funeral Services for Mable Hale Forsey." October 24, 1960. Typewritten copy.

_____. Address given at the 52nd Annual Primary Conference of The Church of Jesus Christ of Latter-day Saints, April 3, 1958.

McConkie, Bruce R. *Mormon Doctrine*. 2nd ed. Salt Lake City: Bookcraft, 1966.

_____. *Doctrinal New Testament Commentary*. 3 vols. Salt Lake City: Bookcraft, 1965–73.

_____. *A New Witness for the Articles of Faith*. Salt Lake City: Deseret Book, 1985.

_____. "The Probationary Test of Mortality." Address given at the Salt Lake Institute of Religion, 10 January 1982.

McConkie, Joseph Fielding and Robert L. Millet. *Joseph Smith, the Choice Seer.* Salt Lake City: Bookcraft, 1996.

*Merriam-Webster's Collegiate Dictionary.* 10th ed. Springfield, Massachusetts: Merriam-Webster, 2000.

Merrill, Joseph F. *The Millennial Star.* Editorial. February 13, 1936. Manchester, London, and Liverpool, England: The Church of Jesus Christ of Latter-day Saints, 1840–1970.

Near-death.com. "The NDE [Near-Death Experiences] and the Silver Cord." Internet website, www.near-death.com/experiences/ research12.html. Accessed November 16, 2010.

Nelson, Russell M. "Doors of Death." *Ensign*, May 1992. Salt Lake City: The Church of Jesus Christ of Latter-day Saints, 1971 to present.

Penrose, Charles W. *Deseret News: Semi-Weekly.* February 28, 1918. Salt Lake City: The Church of Jesus Christ of Latter-day Saints, 1866–1922.

_____. *The Millennial Star.* Editorial. March 14, 1907. Manchester, London, and Liverpool, England: The Church of Jesus Christ of Latter-day Saints, 1840–1970.

Peterson, H. Donl. Quoted in Brian L. Smith's "Joseph Smith: Gifted Learner, Master Teacher, Prophetic Seer." Provo, Utah: Brigham Young University Religious Studies Center, 1993.

Pratt, Orson. *Key to the Science of Theology.* Salt Lake City: Deseret News, 1883.

_____. "Figure and Magnitude of Spirits." *The Seer.* March 1853, vol. 1, no. 2. Washington, DC: The Church of Jesus Christ of Latter-day Saints, 1853–54.

_____. "Questions and Answers on Doctrine." *The Seer.* January 1854, vol. II, no. 1. Washington, DC: The Church of Jesus Christ of Latter-day Saints, 1853–54.

Richards, Franklin D. *Collected Discourses*. 2nd ed. Compiled and edited by Brian H. Stuy. Scarborough, Canada: BHS Publishing, 1986–89.

Roberts, B. H. *Young Woman's Journal*. September 1916, vol. 27. Salt Lake City: The Church of Jesus Christ of Latter-day Saints, 1889–1929.

*Sharing the Gospel with Others, Excerpts from the Sermons of President Smith*. Compiled by Preston Nibley. Salt Lake City: Deseret Book.

Smith, Joseph. *History of The Church of Jesus Christ of Latter-day Saints*. Edited by B. H. Roberts. 7 vols. Salt Lake City: Deseret Book, 1976.

———. *Teachings of the Prophet Joseph Smith*. Selected by Joseph Fielding Smith. Salt Lake City: Deseret Book, 1976.

Smith, Joseph F. *Gospel Doctrine: Selections from the Sermons and Writings of Joseph F. Smith*. Salt Lake City: Deseret Book, 1973.

———. "Personal Letterbooks," page 348, film reel #10; historical department of The Church of Jesus Christ of Latter-day Saints, Ms. F 271.

———. *Young Woman's Journal*. March 1912, vol. 23. Salt Lake City: The Church of Jesus Christ of Latter-day Saints, 1889–1929.

Smith, Joseph Fielding. *Answers to Gospel Questions*. Compiled by Joseph Fielding Smith Jr. 5 vols. Salt Lake City: Deseret Book, 1957–66.

———. *Doctrines of Salvation*. Compiled by Bruce R. McConkie. 3 vols. Salt Lake City: Bookcraft, 1954–56.

———. *Essentials in Church History*. 27th ed. Salt Lake City: Deseret Book, 1974.

———. *Man: His Origin and Destiny*. Salt Lake City: Deseret Book, 1954.

———. *Utah Genealogical and Historical Magazine*. Salt Lake City: Genealogical Society of Utah, 1910–40.

Snow, LeRoi. "Raised from the Dead." *Improvement Era*, October 1929. Salt Lake City: The Church of Jesus Christ of Latter-day Saints, 1897–1970.

Talmage, James E. "The Earth and Man." *The Millennial Star*. December 31, 1931. Manchester, London, and Liverpool, England: The Church of Jesus Christ of Latter-day Saints, 1840–1970.

*Teachings of Presidents of the Church: Wilford Woodruff.* Salt Lake City: The Church of Jesus Christ of Latter-day Saints, 2004.

*The Presidents of the Church.* Edited by Leonard J. Arrington. Salt Lake City: Deseret Book, 1986.

Whitney, Orson F. "A Terrible Ordeal." *Helpful Visions.* 14th vol. in a series. Salt Lake City: Juvenile Instructor Office, 1887.

_____. *The Life of Heber C. Kimball.* 2nd ed. Salt Lake City: Bookcraft, 1945.

_____. *The Millennial Star.* Editorial. January 26, 1922. Manchester, London, and Liverpool, England: The Church of Jesus Christ of Latter-day Saints, 1840–1970

_____. *Young Woman's Journal.* April 1910. Salt Lake City: The Church of Jesus Christ of Latter-day Saints, 1889–1929.

_____. *Young Woman's Journal.* April 1928. Salt Lake City: The Church of Jesus Christ of Latter-day Saints, 1889–1929.

Wikipedia. "World Population." Internet website, http://en.wikipedia.org/wiki/World_population. Accessed November 16, 2010.

_____. "Silver Cord." Internet website, http://en.wikipedia.org/wiki/Silver_cord. Accessed November 16, 2010

_____. "Astral Projection. Internet website, http://en.wikipedia.org/wiki/astral_projection. Accessed November 16, 2010.

Woodruff, Wilford. *The Discourses of Wilford Woodruff.* Selected by G. Homer Durham. Salt Lake City: Bookcraft, 1969.

# INDEX

# ABOUT THE AUTHOR

Bruce E. Dana is an avid student of the gospel, who served as a missionary in the Northwestern States and Pacific Northwest missions for the Church. He attended Weber State College and Utah State University. He has served in a wide variety of Church callings and enjoys teaching the doctrines of the gospel. He is married to Brenda Lamb and is the father of eight children.

Bruce is the author of eight other published LDS doctrinal books. They are *Mysteries of the Kingdom*; *Mary, Mother of Jesus*; *Simon Peter*; *The Three Nephites and Other Translated Beings*; *Glad Tidings Near Cumorah*; *The Eternal Father and His Son*; *The Apostleship*; *The Three Most Important Events: The Vital Roles of the Creation, the Fall and the Atonement In Our Lives*; and the bestselling humor book *Stories & Jokes of Mormon Folks*.